tS·9S

The Esoteric Structure
of Bach's Clavierübung III

The Esoteric Structure of Bach's Clavierübung III

David Humphreys

University College Cardiff Press

First published 1983 in Great Britain by
University College Cardiff Press,
P.O. Box 78, Cardiff, CF1 1XL.

Copyright © 1983 University College Cardiff

British Library Cataloguing in Publication Data
Humphreys, David
    The Esoteric Structure of Bach's Clavierübung III
    1. Bach, Johann Sebastian
    I. Title
    786'.092'4   ML410.B1

ISBN 0-906449-55-3

Printed by J.W. Arrowsmith Ltd., Bristol

iv

Contents

List of Tables

List of Plates

List of Figures

Acknowledgments

It is a pleasure to express my gratitude to Mr. Malcolm Boyd for reading the typescript study with great care and making a number of corrections and valuable suggestions. Any errors that remain are my fault.

I am also indebted to Dr. Ulrich Siegele and (alas, posthumously) to Mr. Peter Opie for detailed and generous responses to my enquiries, to the governing body of the British Library for permission to reproduce the title-pages of the four *Clavierübung* volumes, and to Dr. Michael Robinson for several suggestions.

The proof-reading was kindly undertaken by Mr. Malcolm Boyd and Dr. David Wyn Jones of University College, Cardiff.

D.L.H.

To the memory of my parents

1 – The Traditional View

In September 1739, J.S. Bach published the third of his four great collections of keyboard music under the general title *Clavierübung*. Its title-page runs as follows:

> Dritter Theil der Clavier Übung bestehend in verschiedenen Vorspielen über die Catechismus – und andere Gesaenge, vor die Orgel: Denen Liebhabern, und besonders denen Kennern von dergleichen Arbeit, zur Gemüths Ergezung verfertiget von Johann Sebastian Bach, Koenigl. Pohlnischen, und Churfürstl. Saechss. Hoff-Compositeur, Capell-meister, und Directore Chori Musici in Leipzig. In Verlegung des Authoris.

> Third part of the Clavier Lessons, consisting of various preludes on the Catechism Hymns and other chorales, for organ: composed for amateurs of music, and especially for connoisseurs of such productions, for the recreation of their spirits, by Johann Sebastian Bach, Royal Polish and Electoral Saxon Court Composer, Capellmeister and Choirmaster in Leipzig. Published by the Author.

The volume contains the 27 items listed in Table 1 (see p. 2). It has won universal recognition as one of Bach's major productions in the field of organ music, the superb prelude and fugue and some of the 21 chorale preludes forming part of the standard repertoire of the organist. Naturally, the set has also received much scholarly attention, having been studied closely by writers ranging chronologically from Kirnberger to Peter Williams.[1] This is not surprising, for quite apart from its artistic importance the set raises a number of intriguing questions of which by no means all have been convincingly answered. Most of them concern the ordering of the collection, a subject about which Bach's wording on the title page seems almost deliberately vague; his reference to the 'Catechismus- und andere Gesaenge' certainly gives a clue to the interpretation of some of the chorale preludes, but there are more baffling problems on which Bach remains silent. What is the function of the four Duetti, and how are we to account for their position within the order? What is the purpose of the opening prelude and closing fugue? Did Bach indeed mean

1

them to be played together, and if so why are they so widely separated? Why is each chorale given both *manualiter* and *pedaliter* settings, and why is one chorale (*Allein Gott in der Höh' sei Ehr'*) singled out for *three* settings? If there is, as almost all Bach scholars have concluded, a plan behind the ordering of the

Table 1. The contents of Bach's Clavierübung III

		BWV
1	Praeludium	552 (i)
2	Kyrie, Gott Vater in Ewigkeit I	669
3	Christe, aller Welt Trost I	670
4	Kyrie, Gott heiliger Geist I	671
5	Kyrie, Gott Vater in Ewigkeit II	672
6	Christe, aller Welt Trost II	673
7	Kyrie, Gott heiliger Geist II	674
8	Allein Gott in der Höh' sei Ehr' I	675
9	Allein Gott in der Höh' sei Ehr' II	676
10	Allein Gott in der Höh' sei Ehr' III	677
11	Dies sind die heil'gen zehn Gebot' I	678
12	Dies sind die heil'gen zehn Gebot' II	679
13	Wir glauben all' an einen Gott I	680
14	Wir glauben all' an einen Gott II	681
15	Vater unser im Himmelreich I	682
16	Vater unser im Himmelreich II	683
17	Christ unser Herr zum Jordan kam I	684
18	Christ unser Herr zum Jordan kam II	685
19	Aus tiefer Not schrei' ich zu dir I	686
20	Aus tiefer Not schrei' ich zu dir II	687
21	Jesus Christus unser Heiland I	688
22	Jesus Christus unser Heiland II	689
23	Duetto I	802
24	Duetto II	803
25	Duetto III	804
26	Duetto IV	805
27	Fuga	552 (ii)

Spellings have been modernised. The Roman numerals for 23 – 26 are original; otherwise the numbering (Roman and Arabic) is editorial.

set, why did Bach not specify it more clearly in his title-page? How much of the music was intended for performance within the Lutheran liturgy, and at which services? Writers on Bach have offered various solutions which undoubtedly illuminate some of these problems, but have not succeeded in finding an overall plan which accounts satisfactorily for Bach's ordering as a whole. The purpose of this study is to communicate the discovery of such a plan, which sheds a surprising new light on the whole collection and establishes Bach's *Clavierübung* III as one of the masterpieces of Western esoteric art.

An order for one group of pieces within the set is obvious, and has been almost universally recognised. Items 11 – 22 are a series of preludes in alternative *manualiter* and *pedaliter* settings on six chorales, all by Martin Luther[2] and following the successive articles of Luther's Lesser Catechism as shown in Table 2 (see p. 4).

There is also a 'natural' order for items 2 – 10. Since 2 – 4 and 5 – 7 are alternative settings of a German troped Kyrie, and 8 – 10 of the standard German metrical version of the Gloria, the group can form a Lutheran *Missa brevis*, including the items of the Lutheran Mass most usually subjected to musical setting in Bach's day (notably, of course, in Bach's own concerted 'short' masses). It is possible that these liturgical implications could be pushed slightly further. In Luther's *Deutsche Messe und Ordnung des Gottesdienstes* (Wittenberg, 1526) two alternative forms of German mass are advocated in addition to the traditional Latin form. One is for public worship, celebrated in church, formal, and addressed to all mankind 'just as if we were holding a service among the Turks or heathens in a public place or in the fields'. The other form, called by Luther 'the proper form which the evangelical order should take' is more private, addressed more to the converted and less formal; it should involve 'reading, baptism, taking the sacraments, alms-giving and catechizing'. The identification of Luther's two alternative settings has not won universal acceptance, but the discoveries outlined in the present article provide some support for it.

3

Table 2. The headings of Luther's Lesser Catechism and the opening lines of the Catechism Chorales

Catechism	Chorale
Die zehn Gebote, wie sie ein Hausvater seinem Gesinde einfältiglich vorhalten soll	Dies sind die heil'gen zehn Gebot'
Der Glaube, wie ein Hausvater denselbigen seinem Gesinde aufs einfältigste vorhalten soll	Wir glauben all' an einen Gott
Das Vaterunser, wie dasselbige ein Hausvater seinem Gesinde aufs einfältigste vorhalten soll	Vater unser im Himmelreich
Das Sakrament der heiligen Taufe, wie dasselbige ein Hausvater seinem Gesinde soll einfältig vorhalten	Christ unser Herr zum Jordan kam
Wie man die Einfältigen soll lehren beichten	Aus tiefer Not schrei' ich zu dir
Das Sakrament des Altars, wie ein Hausvater dasselbige einfältiglich vorhalten soll	Jesus Christus unser Heiland

The spellings of the Catechism headings are in accordance with *Martin Luther Ausgewählte Werke*, ed. H.H. Borcherdt and G. Merz, (Munich 1948 –), Vol. III.

Another much-discussed hypothesis is that the *manualiter* and *pedaliter* preludes in the Catechism group refer respectively to Luther's Lesser and Greater Catechisms.

Various factors unifying the group of Mass preludes have been noticed. There are nine preludes, divided into three groups of

4

three (first Kyrie cycle, second Kyrie cycle, Gloria cycle). Trinity symbolism has also been noticed elsewhere in the set, notably in the total number of pieces (27) and in certain features of the final fugue, but it is not stressed in the opposed group of Catechism preludes. Again, whereas all six chorales used for the Catechism preludes are Luther's own versifications, neither of the Mass texts is. The Kyrie is set to the well-known German trope *Gott Vater in Ewigkeit* (an anonymous contrafactum of the Latin trope *Fons bonitatis* first published in 1537)[3] while the Gloria employs the versification by Nikolaus Decius.[4] Both these were used regularly for the celebration of German Mass in centres of Lutheran worship (including the Leipzig churches). However, there is, as several scholars have pointed out, no justification for the use of titles such as German Organ Mass for the set as a whole.

We now come to the four Duetti, extended pieces in contrapuntal two-voice texture which immediately follow the last of the Catechism preludes and precede the final fugue. They pose a considerable problem which no Bach commentator has yet satisfactorily resolved. They have no apparent liturgical significance, and Bach has done nothing to make their function clear. Scholars have explained their presence in various ways; some have suggested that they got in by mistake, some that Bach meant them to be played *sub communione* (this is linked with the 'German Organ Mass' view of the whole set), and some that they are simply miscellaneous pieces designed to make up the total number 27 ($3 \times 3 \times 3$). The number four has suggested connections with the four gospels (Ross), the four elements (Steglich) and the progression Passiontide – Easter – Ascension – Whitsun (Birk). The present study advances an explanation for their presence and function which, it is claimed, supersedes those given above. As well as illuminating the function of the Duetti themselves, it also forms the first step towards the rediscovery of the complex and beautiful esoteric structure of the set, a structure which Bach planned and executed with complete deliberation, which he intended to be accessible to anybody with a little knowledge of the music theory and practice of the ancients, and which

5

has been lost for more than two centuries. We shall begin with the end of Blake's 'golden string'. The explanation for the presence of the four Duetti, as of the twelve Catechism preludes, is to be found in the organisation of Luther's Lesser Catechism.

2 – The Significance of the Duetti

Martin Luther published his two German Catechisms separately in 1529. Their object was to correct the woeful state of ignorance of Christian doctrine among the common people and children, and the inability of ministers to teach it effectively. The plan of the Lesser Catechism[5] may be outlined briefly here. After a preface giving instructions for its use, it proceeds to lay out the Ten Commandments, Creed and Lord's Prayer, the last two broken up into short clauses. There follow sections on baptism, confession, the sacraments, morning and evening blessing, grace before and after meals, and finally a table (*Haustafel*) giving rules for conduct for all classes of person within the Christian order. Each main heading in the doctrinal sections is followed by a question asking its meaning (often simply *Was ist das?*) and then by a short paragraph of explanation designed for the pupil to learn by heart. The plan of the Greater Catechism is similar, except that the sections on confession and the sacraments are in reverse order and the succeeding non-doctrinal portions are omitted. Instead of the question-and-answer method, Luther here follows each clause with an explanation of considerable length, almost amounting to a homily.

Now it is clear from Bach's order for the 'communion' and 'confession' preludes that he took the Lesser, rather than the Greater Catechism as his model for the preludes in the Catechism group. Surely therefore the natural procedure is to examine the sections of this Catechism not covered by Bach's preludes in the hope that they might shed some light on other items in the *Clavierübung*. As soon as we adopt this course, we make the first of the discoveries which lead to the esoteric structure. The preface to the Lesser Catechism begins by lamenting the doctrinal ignorance displayed by the common people, and by exhorting pastors and preachers to give them due instruction. There follow four rules designed to help the minister in the task of instilling the Catechism into his pupils. It is, to say the least, surprising that

7

nobody seems to have investigated the possibility that Bach's four Duetti are linked with Luther's four teaching precepts. In the following paragraphs I propose to conduct this investigation, which leads to the conclusion that this was indeed Bach's intention.

Bach's choice of the duo is significant in itself. The well-known didactic associations of the duo or *bicinium* for voices or instruments date back to the early sixteenth century, when a revival of interest in music as an educative force was fostered, for different if not unrelated reasons, by humanist scholars and early Protestants. The classic examples of the didactic teacher-pupil duo, the *Bicinia* of Lassus, enjoyed especial popularity in Germany. Native contributions to the genre included the *bicinia* of Georg Rhau (interestingly enough a close friend of Luther), Caspar Othmayr and Praetorius.[6] The form represents the teacher-pupil relationship in two ways, first in the purely practical sense that one performer can take each part, and secondly in the figurative sense that the devices naturally suggested by the form – imitation, canon and (later) fugue – form a didactic symbol. One voice 'teaches' the subject to the other. The duo was still popular in the eighteenth century, and examples by Telemann, W.F. Bach and C.P.E. Bach found a ready market, as did a large number of 'equal-voiced' duos in other countries. Bach's choice of it here gives a clue to his intentions; in the metaphorical form of duos for one instrument only the Duetti depict the relationship between the teacher and the taught.

But in the key-sequence of the four movements Bach has left a second, more concrete clue, which, although undoubtedly intended to be understood by at least some of his readers, has long since been lost sight of. The Duetti are respectively in E minor, F major, G major and A minor, keys whose tonic triads form an ascending 'white-note' stepwise progression (Ex. 1).

Ex. 1.

Readers with an interest in the music theory of the ancients would not have missed the point of this. The octave scale e – e′ formed by the four triads is nothing other than the central Dorian octave species in the ancient Greek (Ptolemaic) fifteen-note system in the Dorian tonos (Ex. 2).

Ex. 2.

The two disjunct tetrachords of which the octave species is composed (bracketed in the example) are given respectively by the four triadic roots and the four fifths, thus preventing any possibility of confusion with the invertible fifth species and fourth species of the Gregorian system. Moreoever the arrangement of major and minor keys (minor, major, major, minor) is organised so that the four triadic thirds will form part of the required 'white-note' scale.

The standard classical exposition of the structure of the fifteen-note system is in Ptolemy's *Harmonics* Book II, or its transmission by Boethius and others. But for the classically minded student the next step would be to inquire into the ethical significance of the Dorian mode to the ancients. The fullest treatment of it can be found in the famous passage on music in Plato's *Republic*, a chapter which had been part of the common coin of theoretical discussion for centuries before Bach's use of it. In the following extract the Platonic Socrates, speaking in the first person, closely questions his musician pupil on which modes are most suited to producing the required moral qualities in the young citizen:

'Will you make any use of [the Ionian and Lydian modes] for warriors?' 'None at all,' he said, 'but it would seem that you have left the Dorian and the Phrygian.' 'I don't know the harmonies,' I said, 'but leave me that harmony that would fittingly imitate the utterances and the accents of a brave man who is engaged in warfare or in any enforced business, and who, when he has failed, either meeting wounds or death or having fallen into some other mishap, in all these conditions confronts fortune with steadfast endurance and repels her strokes. And another for such a man engaged in works of peace, not enforced but voluntary, either trying to persuade somebody of something and imploring him – whether it be a god, through prayer, or a man, by teaching and admonition – or contrariwise yielding himself to another who is petitioning or teaching him or trying to change his opinions, and in consequence faring according to his wish, and not bearing himself arrogantly, but in all this acting modestly and moderately and acquiescing in the outcome. Leave us these two harmonies – the enforced and the voluntary – that will best imitate the utterances of men failing or succeeding, the temperate, the brave – leave us these.'[7]

Plato does not specify which qualities belong to which of his two recommended modes, but the interpretation given to this classic passage by Western tradition identified the mode for 'a brave man who is engaged in warfare' with the Phrygian and the gentle, persuasive, didactic second mode with the Dorian.[8] This Dorian mode, adapted for 'teaching and admonition' is employed by Bach in the key-sequence of the four Duetti to depict the relationship between master and pupil.

This, then, is how Bach links the general plan of the Duetti with the four teaching precepts from the preface of Luther's Lesser Catechism. These precepts are placed immediately before the doctrinal sections of the Catechism which dictates the plan of Bach's chorale preludes. Like the precepts, Bach's Duetti are four in number, and they contain clues deliberately planted by the composer to indicate that they portray the teacher-pupil relationship, which is treated verbally by Luther. Thus the Duetti, unexplained until now, drop neatly into place as part of the overall plan of the whole set.

This raises the question: is there a specific connection between the individual pieces and the individual rules? That there is such a connection can be established by Bach's use of the humanist verbal symbolism which played a highly important role in eighteenth-century German music theory[9] and, as Ursula Kirkendale has shown in an article of major importance,[10] is central to the inner ordering of Bach's Musical Offering. Its guiding principle, derived from the ideals of Horace, Cicero and Quintilian by the sixteenth-century humanist scholars who inaugurated a line of thought which remained unbroken in the Leipzig of Bach's day, is the orator's art of communication. Its standard device is word-painting, which adds a layer of expressive ornament to an idea from the text and enhances its power to move the audience. The figure does not convey the inner idea in an impressionistic sense, but 'stands for' it in ways which, on analysis, prove to have surprisingly obscure and complex psychological roots. In the Duetti the esoteric element lies not in the symbolism itself, but in the fact that the text which it elaborates is not stated, but has to be divined from the clues explained above. In the following exposition, we shall take the Duetti in order.

Duetto I (23)

Luther's first rule warns the preacher against varying the form of words used for the Creed, Commandments, Lord's Prayer and other standard religious texts.

> First, that above all the preacher should take good care not to use now one, now another text and form of the Ten Commandments, Lord's Prayer, Creed, Sacraments etc., but take to his use a single form, keeping to it and urging it constantly year after year. For silly young folk have to be taught a single unchanging text and form, otherwise they easily go astray.
> No doubt this was also apparent to the Church Fathers, who used the Lord's Prayer, Creed, and Ten Commandments in a single form. Therefore we too should teach such things to simple young folk without displacing as much as a syllable, or presenting and pronouncing them differently one year from the last.
> So pick out the form you wish, and keep to it always. However, when you preach to the learned and those with understanding you may show your art and elaborate these texts in as colourful and ingenious a manner as you wish. But with young folk keep to a fixed, unchanging form and wording, and begin by teaching them the following portions: the Ten Commandments, the Creed, the Lord's Prayer etc., following the text word for word so that they can say it after you and know it by heart. . . . [11]

Appropriately, Bach's Duetto I is a relatively straightforward piece somewhat in the manner of the two-part inventions; its main material is a pair of themes in double counterpoint appearing four times in each permutation. The most immediately recognisable feature of the upper voice is its opening rising and falling scale, which is first heard unaccompanied (Ex. 3). [12]

Ex. 3. BWV 802, bars 1 – 5.

The behaviour of this scale is interesting; the ascending form has the sharpened sixth and seventh degrees of the melodic minor scale, but here the sharpened degrees are retained for the descending form also. Bach normally showed more respect for convention in his treatment of scale patterns; a good example of his normal practice is the opening of the Chromatic Fantasia and Fugue BWV 903 (Ex. 4).

Ex. 4. BWV 903, bars 1 – 2.

Not only does the unconventional scale pattern in Duetto I appear at the opening of each entry, but also as a feature of one of the principal episodic ideas (bars 18 – 21) in which the scale is heard in canon at a bar's distance. Finally, from the fourth entry (bars 29 – 35) onwards, the scale, originally unaccompanied, now appears accompanied by itself in close canon (Ex. 5).

Ex. 5. BWV 802, bars 29 – 31.

This canonic elaboration of the scale appears in all subsequent entries, testifying to the aptitude of the pupil. The scale is to be identified with the text discussed in Luther's first injunction – the text which the pupil is to learn by heart and which the teacher is to keep in an unvaried wording 'without displacing as much as a syllable' – that is, in Bach's terms, without altering the sixth and seventh degrees even to allow for the normal movement of the melodic minor form.

Duetto II (24)

Luther's second rule is brief enough to quote in full.

When they know the text well, then teach them understanding also, so that they know its meaning. And repeatedly take up the commentary given in these tables (or another short commentary, whichever you like) and keep to it without altering a syllable, taking the commentary applicable to the text. For it is not necessary that you should undertake all the portions together, but rather one after the other. Once they understand the first commandment well, then take up the second, and so forth; otherwise they become overloaded, so that they remember nothing well.

Having learnt the text, the pupil learns its meaning, either through the medium of Luther's Catechism, or through 'sonst eine kurze einige Weise'. The key to the understanding of the link between Luther's teaching and Duetto II lies in the word *Verstand*; the teaching of 'understanding' is also the purpose of Bach's Duetto II.

Duetto II is radically different in character from Duetto I. It is a strict fugue and abounds in all kinds of contrapuntal artifice. The first episode (bars 10 – 17) is a canon at the tenth below, taken up again in a modified form at bars 22 – 26. Shortly afterwards (bars 37 – 53) there follows another canon, this time at the

13

compound fourth below, which then immediately inverts to form a canon at the twelfth above (bars 52 – 66). The first eight bars of this canon are intervallically strict (bars 37, last quaver – 45) and the last eight (bars 46 – 53) composed within the diatonic scale and forming a stretto entry of the main subject. The intervallic canon, though bizarre in effect, forms a vivid illustration of the pupil following the labyrinthine twists of his master's reasoning (Ex. 6).

Ex. 6. BWV 803, bars 37 – 45.

Thirdly (bars 69 – 73) Bach reintroduces the main subject in the tonic with a chromatic countersubject and then immediately inverts the whole combination melodically (mirror writing) in the following five bars. Finally the whole piece is circular, at least in the visual or notational sense that the score ends with a *dal segno* to bar 5. The connection of all this with Luther's second precept needs no further elaboration.

Duetto III (25)

When the Lesser Catechism has been learnt and understood, says Luther's third rule, the teacher should take the Greater Catechism and add still further to the pupil's understanding of the religious texts:

14

When you have taught them this short Catechism, then take up the long Catechism and enrich and broaden their understanding. At this point concentrate in turn on each commandment, petition and portion with its manifold effects, applications, benefits, dangers and penalties, as you will find it all in plenty in so many booklets on the subject. And in particular, urge most strongly the commandment and portion of which your congregation stands in most need. For instance, you must vigorously urge the seventh commandment on stealing upon manual workers, tradesmen, and indeed also upon peasants and servants, for with such folk all kinds of dishonesty and thievery are rife. Also, you must urge the fourth commandment well upon children and men of low degree, for them to be quiet, honest, obedient and peaceable, and always introduce many examples from Scripture of how God blesses and chastises such people . . .

The application of this rule to Bach's Duetto III requires some thought. Clearly we are not concerned here with 'manual workers, tradesmen . . . peasants and servants' but (in view of the didactic aims of the Duetti in general) with 'children and men of low degree' – especially with children. Bach has therefore obeyed Luther's injunction to the preacher and composed a piece which is nothing less than a musical portrayal of the familiar words: 'Honour thy father and mother, that thy days may be long in the land which the Lord thy God giveth thee'. In Luther's language, Bach is 'urging the fourth commandment well upon children and men of low degree, for them to be quiet honest, obedient and peaceable'.

Duetto III is much simpler in construction than Duetto II, and has a warmth and lyricism which contrasts pleasantly with the brittle virtuosity of the latter. Its most immediately striking feature is its gentle 12/8 metre; pre-eminently the metre of the siciliano, it is often associated in Bach's music (at least in major keys) with sentiments of pastoral tranquillity.[13] In Duetto III, Bach uses it to convey the idea of peace in two senses: first, as the peaceable (*friedsam*) bearing of children towards their parents, and secondly as the promised repose of 'the land which the Lord thy God giveth thee'.

The opening, which supplies all the thematic material, is shown in Ex. 7.

Ex. 7. BWV 804, bars 1 – 2.

The gracious, curtseying figures (one for each parent!) of the first part of the subject (RH) portray the first part of the injunction; with their deferential downward movement they are indeed 'quiet, honest, obedient and peaceable'. To grasp the meaning of the flowing stream of semiquavers which form the other element we have to recall the familiar biblical metaphor for 'the land which the Lord thy God giveth thee'. The phrase 'a land flowing with milk and honey' occurs in some form or other in nearly twenty biblical contexts, and by representing it here by a gently flowing stream of semiquavers Bach has followed Luther's instruction to introduce examples from the Scriptures. The flow of milk and honey pursues a fairly quiet course through most of the piece, but towards the end of it broadens into something approaching a torrent (bars 30 – 33, quoted in Ex. 8):

Ex. 8. BWV 804, bars 30 – 33.

Duetto IV (26)

Luther's fourth and last teaching precept is a warning to those who mistakenly imagine that they can, under the reformed order, afford to neglect the sacraments:

Because the tyranny of the Pope is now at an end, they will no longer visit the sacrament and hold it in scorn. For all that you must urge it strongly, but note this: we must never compel anybody to believe or take the sacrament, or impose a rule as to time and place, but preach in such a way that they discipline themselves and immediately compel us, the priests, to administer the sacrament. We can do this by telling them: If anybody does not visit or desire the sacrament at least once or four times a year, that signifies that he despises the sacrament and is no Christian . . . .

If anybody pays little heed to the sacrament, that is a sign that he does not acknowledge sin, the flesh, the devil, the world, death, peril and hell, that is, he believes in nothing, although he is up to his ears in it, and is doubly of the Devil. Likewise he may not expect grace, life, paradise, heaven, Christ, God or any good. For if he believed that he had all this evil and lacked all this good, he would not so neglect the sacrament by which all this evil is remedied and all this good is given. Even him we should not compel by rule to visit the sacrament, but he himself should come running helter-skelter (*gelaufen und gerennet*), discipline himself and urge you that you should give him the sacrament.

The course of action prescribed is clear. The preacher is not to impose a law of attendance, but should tell his flock in no uncertain terms that if they refuse or neglect the sacraments they are 'doubly of the Devil'. If the preacher employs the full force of his eloquence, the errant members should come 'gelaufen und gerennet' to the Communion rail.

Bach's Duetto IV is a regular fugue on the following remarkable subject (Ex. 9).

Ex. 9. BWV 805, bars 1 – 8.

17

It falls into two sections, the first of weirdly angular cut and the second a *perpetuum mobile* in quavers. To examine the first component more closely: it begins by outlining the A minor triad and then seems to lose its tonal bearings, moving first to an implied subdominant at bar 3, and then, via the cadential F♯ to an implied cadence in G minor, before being wrenched back to the tonic by the G♯ at the end of bar 4. Also worthy of note is the aimless succession of upward and downward movement (up to the beginning of bar 5 there are no fewer than six changes of direction). Finally, even the rhythm wanders from the straight and narrow, supporting the metrical accents in bars 1 – 2 and straying into syncopations in bars 3 – 4. That is, all three elements in the conventional eighteenth-century division of music (melody, harmony, rhythm) are used to express errancy, just as all three contribute to the return to the chosen path in the second component. This restores stability with an iron hand by an immediate return to the tonic which is then hammered home with simple harmony circling narrowly round the tonic chord. The analogy with the preacher's desired effect on the scoffers castigated by Luther could hardly be more exact. Having strayed like the wandering sheep of biblical metaphor, they hear the stern warnings of the preacher and come running back to the fold of the tonic key to the accompaniment of Bach's scurrying quavers. Again, the choice of the fugue form (*fuga* = flight) is surely no coincidence.

It appears then that both generally and specifically the four Duetti are intended to portray the instruction of the Lutheran pupil according to the precepts laid out by Luther in the preface to the Lesser Catechism. The connection is established in general by clues hidden in the key-sequence, and, quite simply, by the didactic symbolism to connect each of the four pieces with one precept. The discovery has one more consequence whose implications will be fully discussed later. The four Duetti must now be included within the orbit of the Catechism preludes, which now form part of a larger group of not twelve but sixteen pieces.

3 – The Significance of the Prelude and Fugue

The prelude and fugue, like the Duetti, have long presented a seemingly intractable problem. They too seem to have no place within the general liturgical plan of the collection. Organists have generally regarded them (correctly, as we shall see) as belonging together, but why has Bach placed them so far apart? In spite of their identity of key, the considerable length of both pieces and the lack of any specific indication from Bach that they belong together have led at least one Bach commentator to the conclusion that the pairing may be a mistake.[14]

The first indication that it is not comes, once more, from Luther. Following the discovery that the Duetti, like the Catechism preludes, are related to Luther's Lesser Catechism, it is only natural to seek a place within the Catechism for the prelude and fugue also. The last portion of the Catechism used by Bach for the chorale preludes is headed *Das Sakrament des Altars*, and following it is another inscribed *Wie ein Hausvater sein Gesinde soll lehren, morgens und abends sich segnen.*

Luther's instructions for morning and evening blessing are short, and may be quoted both in the original and in translation. First, the morning blessing:

Des Morgens, so du aus dem Bette fährest, sollst du dich segnen mit dem heiligen Kreuz und sagen: Des walt Gott Vater, Sohn, heiliger Geist, Amen.	In the morning, when you get up, you are to bless yourself with the Holy Cross and say, In the name of God the Father, the Son and the Holy Ghost, Amen.

The pupil then says the Creed and Lord's Prayer and, if he wishes, a morning collect given by Luther.

The evening blessing is the same:

Des Abends, wenn du zu Bette gehest, sollst du sich segnen mit dem heiligen Kreuz und sagen: Das walt Gott Vater, Sohn, heiliger Geist, Amen.	In the evening, when you go to bed, you are to bless yourself with the Holy Cross and say, In the name of God the Father, the Son and the Holy Ghost, Amen.

also followed by the Creed and Lord's Prayer, with an optional collect.

Within these two momentous instructions is contained the key to the understanding of the geometric microcosm which Bach placed at the heart of the esoteric design of the whole collection. The discovery of this design must wait for a later section. For the moment, we shall content ourselves by examining the two opposed types of Trinity symbolism which link the prelude and fugue with the Trinitarian blessing. For this is indeed the function of the prelude and fugue within the plan of the whole collection; placed appropriately at the beginning and end of the series, they represent, respectively, the morning blessing with which the Lutheran day opens and the evening blessing with which it closes.

The idea that the prelude (1) is intended to portray the three Persons of the Trinity is by no means new; it was proposed in 1974 by Chailley. [15] However, Chailley's detailed examination of the symbolism does not seem to penetrate Bach's intentions to the full, and it therefore seems appropriate to submit the prelude to a re-examination. It is built from three contrasted blocks of material (bars $1 - 32^3$, $32^4 - 51^1$ and $71^1 - 98^3$), hereinafter referred to as A, B and C. Chailley correctly identifies these respectively with the Father, the Son and the Holy Spirit.

The identification of the A sections with the God the Father rests on an idea which Kirkendale's study of the Musical Offering[16] has made familiar; the dotted rhythms, and in particular the paeon rhythm ♩ ♫♫♩ with which the piece opens, are features of the French overture, having served in Lully's hands as expressive symbols of the majesty of the Sun King. In Bach's hands they portray the regality of God the Father. Bach employs a similar device in the *manualiter* prelude on *Wir glauben all'* (14).

In the Jesus music (B) the symbolism is richer and more detailed. The opening of its first statement is quoted in Ex. 10.

Ex. 10. BWV 552(i), bars 31 – 40.

The idea consists of a short phrase followed by an exact repetition in the form of an echo effect, the whole passage then being repeated a fifth higher. How is this connected with God the Son? Simply by the orthodox theological view of Christ as Image of God. The idea is simplicity itself; the echoed repetitions are, in the language of the Creed, 'one in substance' with the initial statements. Furthermore, it is impossible not to notice that the idea itself is 'begotten of the Father' in the sense that the opening motif springs from the principal idea of the A material (Ex. 11).

Ex. 11. BWV 552(i).

Finally, as the continuation makes clear, the descending motion of the B theme, and especially the heavy landing on the thudding low pedal notes, depicts Christ's descent into generation.

The continuation (bars 40 – 50) is equally rich in meaning, and had better be quoted in full (Ex. 12).

Ex. 12. BWV 552(i), bars 40 – 49.

The first four bars of the extract (bars 40⁴ – 44 of the entire piece) employ the alternating *alla zoppa* and Pyrrhic rhythms which Bach was to employ again eight years later in the Musical Offering. Ursula Kirkendale's admirable illumination of their function in this later work can also be applied here.[17] The urgent *alla zoppa* figure, alternating with the warlike Pyrrhicius rhythm to form the aggregate preceived by the ear as

is intended to represent battle. In the Musical Offering it depicts the verbal struggle between the orator and his opponents; here it represents Christ's struggle with the forces of evil, following on naturally from the 'incarnation' idea.

The *alla zoppa* rhythm is still prominent in the second part of the extract (complete piece bars 45 – 50), but there is nevertheless a pronounced change in the character of the upper voice. It is in the pathetic, affective style of the aria. The languishing chromatic inflections, syncopations and appoggiaturas are familiar from countless florid arias from Bach's cantatas and Passions; one example amongst scores of others is the following from Cantata 182 (Ex. 13).[18]

Ex. 13. BWV 182, No. 6, bars 39 – 44.

As the music of the human voice, the aria is the music of Man, showing Christ in his human aspect. Moreover the poignant angularity of the melody, and in particular the sudden turn to the minor, are obvious expressions of pathos, introduced as a portrayal of his Passion and crucifixion.

The esoteric programme of the whole section can now be summed up: Christ is the Image of God, begotten of the Father; he descends into generation to do battle with the forces of darkness, to become man, and to undergo suffering.

This section is followed by an altered recapitulation of the God the Father music (A) which occupies bars 51 – 71. The most immediately striking change is the rescoring. The main theme, originally stated in the uppermost voice, is now in the tenor,

23

remaining in this position until bar 59, when it switches to the alto. Certain details in the texture, such as the short-lived soprano imitation in bars 52 – 3 which is suddenly cut off by a rushing two-octave descending scale, serve to underline the significance of this; the God the Father music is now 'on earth' as a result of the incarnation of Christ (Ex. 14).

Ex. 14. BWV 552(i) bars 51 – 4.

The Holy Spirit music (C) consists of an extended fugal development of the following subject (Ex. 15).

Ex. 15. BWV 552(i) bars 71 – 2 (extract).

There are several examples in Bach's organ music of the portrayal of the Holy Spirit by rushing semiquavers, but here it is possible to be still more specific. The New Testament uses three principal metaphors in connection with the Holy Spirit. First, the wind: either the wind that 'bloweth where it listeth' (*John* 3,8) or the 'rushing mighty wind' heard by the Apostles before the manifestation of the Spirit at Pentecost (*Acts* 2,2). Second, the 'cloven tongues like as of fire' which descend on the Apostles on the same occasion (*Acts* 2,3). Third, the descending dove mentioned in all four Gospels[19] as a metaphor for the descent of the Spirit which follows Christ's baptism in the Jordan. The first of these metaphors is suggested in general by the fluid, swirling semi-quaver motion, but the references to the other two are more specific; the descending dove and the tongues of fire appear, respectively, in the descending scale and the flickering semiquavers which form the two elements of the subject.

But this is not all. Bach's 'Holy Spirit', in the language of the Nicene Creed, 'proceeds from the Father and the Son together'. The procedure from 'the Father' is melodic, extending the downward-moving figure with which the prelude opens (Ex. 16).

Ex. 16. BWV 552(i).

The procedure from 'the Son' is rhythmic, taking its point of departure from the characteristic syncopated rhythm of the 'martial' subsidiary theme in B (beginning bar 40^4). This derivation is shown in Ex. 17.

Ex. 17. BWV 552(i).

Turning now to the fugue (27) we present its contrasting numerical Trinity symbolism in Table 3 (p. 27). Much of it is already familiar, though the significance of the bar-multiples has not, it seems, been pointed out before.

Bach's immediate intention in designing the prelude and fugue is fairly obvious; the prelude expresses three Persons, the fugue, one God. The two opposed types of symbolism they represent – verbal and numerical – are only our first encounter with a dualism which runs right through the esoteric design of the *Clavierübung*. The opposition of the two ideals – the one reflecting the human ideals of communication, the other aimed at drawing the hearer into passive contemplation of the order and harmony of the universe – is a familiar feature of the artistic thought of the West from its earliest beginnings in the ancient world.[29] The first (already referred to in connection with the Duetti) is the art of the rhetorician whose skill is directed towards swaying, moving, or 'acting on' his audience. The second is the Platonist ideal, with its aim of elevating the soul to successive degrees of perfection by the passive contemplation of order, harmony, and beauty. The first, the gestural, mimetic art of the orator, is an application of the precepts of Cicero and Quintilian, the second a musical expression of Pythagoreanism (of which more will be said in the following section). Which terms Bach used to describe these two opposed ideals is not certain. Mattheson devoted a section to the second in *Der vollkommene Capellmeister* (1739) ('On Gesticulation') labelling it *hypocritica*. In the present study the two types will be referred to as *musica arithmetica* and *musica oratorica*.

Although word and number are the principal means of expressing this opposition in the prelude and fugue, there is another which is worth noting, as this too has wider implications for the set as a whole. This is the opposition of styles. The prelude is composed in the extrovert *style galant* which was then at the height of its popularity in progressive musical circles in Berlin and Dresden. The square-cut phrasing, light textures, breezy dotted rhythms and sighing feminine endings pay unmistakable tribute to the two Graun brothers and Hasse, all three of whom Bach is recorded as having known and admired. But the fugue inhabits a different world. It is almost the classic instance of Bach's developing taste for *stile antico* counterpoint in the Italian choral and theoretical tradition. This opposition of tastes, too, is drawn into the antithesis which is central to the whole work. We shall see

Table 3. The Trinity Symbolism in the Fugue

Flats in key-signature			3
Subjects			3
Sections			3
Staves per system			3
Systems per page			3

Bar totals

Section 1	36	$(3 \times 3 \times 4)$	4
Section 2	45	$(3 \times 3 \times 5)$	5
Section 3	36	$(3 \times 3 \times 4)$	4
Total	117	$(3 \times 3 \times 13)$	

4 and 5 → 9 (3×3); 5 and 4 → 9 (3×3)

Polyphonic voices

Section 1	5
Section 2	4
Section 3	5

5 and 4 → 9 (3×3); 4 and 5 → 9 (3×3)

Polyphonic voices added to bar multiples

5	+	4	=	9	(3×3)
4	+	5	=	9	(3×3)
5	+	4	=	9	(3×3)

Proportions to *integer* *valor*	Section 1	dupla (alla breve)	2/1
	Section 2	tripla	3/1
	Section 3	sesquialtera	3/2

Entries of principal subject	Section 1	12	
	Section 2	6	
	Section 3	9	
	Total	27	$(3 \times 3 \times 3)$

later that Bach had an overriding reason for placing a piece in progressive taste first in the collection, and nothing else in the set goes quite as far in this direction. In general, the preludes *oratorica* are in Bach's normal High Baroque idiom, with its fusion of elements from the concerto, overture, aria and suite. In the *arithmetica* preludes Bach has much recourse to the *stile antico*, notably in the cantus firmus setting and quasi-choral polyphony of the three preludes forming the greater Kyrie cycle (2 − 4).[21]

We can now identify the *oratorica* and *arithmetica* groups. It is clear from the unification of the Duetti with the Catechism preludes to form a single entity that the *Clavierübung* has a fourfold order: Prelude, Mass, Catechism, Fugue. Furthermore, our identification of the prelude and fugue with Luther's morning and evening doxology adds another dimension, showing that this order is nothing less than a diurnal cycle. Even the Catechism preludes stand for a service in the Lutheran liturgy; the discovery of the diurnal ordering of the set must be seen as a confirmation of Robin Leaver's suggestion that they stand for the Sunday afternoon Vespergottesdienst, in which catechising the young played a central role. Liturgically the set represents the religious exercise for a Lutheran Sunday with the Mass as the major morning celebration. The full implications of this will be discussed later, but the point which immediately concerns us here is that the Mass preludes (2 − 10) are composed as *arithmetica*, the Vesper preludes with Duetti (11 − 26) as *oratorica*. This implies not only that the Mass preludes rely on numerical and geometrical devices and the Catechism preludes on verbal imagery, but the almost equally important negative face of the same principle. There is no verbal symbolism in the Mass preludes, or numerical symbolism in the Catechism preludes. We can thus dispense with many of the more irresponsible numerical speculations which have bedevilled much writing on the Catechism preludes. The fact that so much literature on Bach constantly presents as established fact relationships which could easily have been arrived at by manipulating the digits in a telephone number is doubly regrettable since it only serves to obscure a nucleus of truth. Bach *was* deeply interested in number symbolism, and in the esoteric structure of the *Clavierübung* he

28

employed it with a clarity, elegance and precision which makes fanciful speculation superfluous. The *arithmetica* and *oratorica* sections also represent a fundamental antithesis of ideas and cultural traditions. We have already seen that the word-music section of the *Clavierübung* (that is, the Catechism preludes and the Duetti) are elaborations of the ideas in a classic Lutheran text, namely Luther's Lesser Catechism of 1529. The numerical concepts in the number-music section (the Mass preludes) were so much a part of Western tradition that it would be hazardous to identify them unequivocally with a single text, but the work which represents the epitome of Pythagorean lore and philosophy and to which later writers most constantly refer is the *Timaeus* of Plato, a book which exerted a dominant influence on the Western view of music, cosmology, architecture and other subjects for centuries. The conjunction of these two systems of thought is perfectly logical, since the two civilisations and intellectual systems they represent (pagan and Christian, ancient and modern, Graeco-Roman and Germanic), simply add new depth and richness to the central antithesis of ideas which lies at the heart of the esoteric structure. The next step is to examine the 21 preludes of the Mass and Catechism groups, showing the esoteric element and relating it to its background.

4 – Musica arithmetica
(The Mass Preludes)

Even if the present writer were qualified to attempt it, this short study would be no place for a systematic exposition of the Pythagorean – Platonic intellectual system. For an excellent and thorough discussion (related to Renaissance literature) of the implications, scope and influence of the concept that 'all things are number' the reader may safely be referred to the treatment of the subject of S.K. Heiniger Jr.[22] The commonplace that number, proportion and harmony are the soul of the universe, stated in classic form in the *Timaeus* of Plato, was developed and expanded in multifarious directions by Plotinus Macrobius, Augustine, Boethius, and a multitude of other writers. They ensured for it a place as one of the commonplaces of Western thought, embracing cosmology, music, geometry, theology, mathematics, architecture, medicine and even poetry. The harmonising effect of music itself was generally conceived as a reconciliation of the human microcosm (*musica humana*) with the macrocosmic harmony of the universe (*musica mundana*). Moreover Pythagorean concepts were still part of the normal thought-habits of music theorists of the seventeenth and eighteenth centuries. Proportion theory was a central preoccupation of Robert Fludd, Athanasius Kircher and Andreas Werckmeister, and Fux was following a well-established tradition (represented, for example, by Zarlino (1558) and Morley (1597)) when he devoted most of Part I of *Gradus ad Parnassum* (1725) to a thorough exposition of proportion theory related to the basic musical consequences. It was a tradition which formed a central part of the education of Bach and his readers.

As a prelude to our discussion of Bach's application of these simple, universal proportions to his esoteric structure, it may be useful to reproduce in summary the account of the creation of the universe according to these simple, all-embracing types from the

Timaeus, a work which Bach undoubtedly knew well and which forms the best exposition of the numerical world-order Bach intended to depict. For a detailed exegesis of the crabbed, telescopic text of the original, the reader is referred to the admirable translation and commentary by Cornford[23] to which repeated reference will be made in this section. For this summary, however, it seems best to give a free paraphrase of the original.

Stage 1. The material of the World-Soul, compounded of Sameness, Difference and Existence, is divided into seven parts in proportions derived from the numbers 1, 2, 3 as follows: 1, 2, 3, $2^2, 3^2, 2^3, 3^3$ (or 1, 2, 3, 4, 9, 8, 27). Although Plato himself seems to have visualised this process as the marking-off of a strip into seven portions, later writers such as Crantor and Chalcidius (the latter's version being of particular significance as the form in which the work was transmitted to the mediaeval world)[24] regarded it as a twofold radiation from the generative non-number 1. This was traditionally represented by the 'lambda diagram' (Fig. 1).

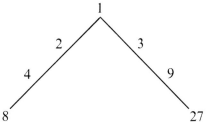

Fig. 1. Lambda Diagram

Stage 2. Between consecutive terms of the two multiplying series 1, 2, 4, 8 and 1, 3, 9, 27 the Demiurge adds the harmonic and arithmetical means. Since some terms appear in both series, the result contains not nineteen, but the following fifteen terms:

1, $\frac{4}{3}$, $\frac{3}{2}$, 2, $\frac{8}{3}$, 3, 4, $\frac{9}{2}$, $\frac{16}{3}$, 6, 8, 9, $\frac{27}{2}$, 18, 27

which can be expressed in integers as

6, 8, 9, 12, 16, 18, 24, 27, 32, 36, 48, 54, 81, 108, 162.

Stage 3. This is best understood if we interpret the arithmetical ratios given above as musical intervals (it is of course essential to the Platonist concept of creation that these relationships are all-pervasive). The result of applying the Stage 2 series to the 'sounding numbers' is shown in Ex. 18.

Ex. 18.

We can now approach the third stage, which adds the intervening ratios needed to fill in the intervals of a complete diatonic scale of four octaves and a major sixth (Ex. 19).

Ex. 19.

After this final division, in Plato's words, 'the mixture from which he was cutting off these portions was used up'.

Bach uses this scheme as a framework against which to project his number structures. The third stage, already represented in the diatonic scale itself, needs no special representation in the esoteric structure, but Bach includes the first two, as well as elements from Pythagorean number symbolism and elaborations from later Neoplatonist writers to produce an astonishingly complete 'type or copy' of the Pythagorean universe. It is important to bear in mind that the numerical devices, which are not especially complex in themselves, have to be treated not in isolation, but as mystic statements referring to aspects of the cosmos as a whole.

A central feature of the numerology of the *Clavierübung* is Bach's inclusion of all three types of proportion encompassed in Plato's system and generally regarded as 'classical' – arithmetical, geometric and harmonic. Some readers may wish to be reminded of the meaning of these terms. In arithmetical proportion the difference between each term and the next is constant (1, 3, 5, 7 . . .). In geometric proportion it is the *ratio* between successive terms which remains constant (3, 6, 12, 24 . . .). Finally, in harmonic or musical progression, the ratio between the first term and the third in a series *a*, *b*, *c* is expressed:

$$a : c = (b - a) : (c - b)$$

In the harmonic progression 3, 4, 6 this ratio is 1 : 2.

The computing of arithmetical, geometric and harmonic means between two numbers was a standard exercise of elementary mathematics, but it also had mystical overtones. The mean term, binding together the otherwise unrelated first and third, was felt as a profound allegory of the cosmic creative and harmonising process, as Bach was well aware.

In the following discussion the three constituent parts of the Mass cycle (greater Kyrie cycle, lesser Kyrie cycle, Gloria cycle) will be taken in order.

Greater Kyrie cycle (2 – 4). The structural basis of all three movements (corresponding to Kyrie I, Christe, Kyrie II) is the chant of the Kyrie trope *Fons bonitatis* in the German contrafactum *Gott Vater in Ewigkeit – Aller Welt Trost – Gott heiliger Geist* in which each clause is addressed to one of the three Persons of the Trinity. The chant appears in the soprano (Kyrie I), tenor (Christe) and bass (Kyrie II) as a cantus firmus in short segments broken up by rests against a background of *stile antico* counterpoint in the accompanying voices. All this is straightforward enough; what has not been noticed is that the durations of the entries and rests are organised according to two related three-term series in harmonic and arithmetical proportions (cf. *Timaeus* Stage 2). The rules are as follows. First, any bar which contains a note of chant is counted as a full bar within the entry. Secondly, the final note in each movement counts as a conventional two-breve long, even though its actual duration on the score may be greater. Thirdly, at the opening of Kyrie II it is necessary to take the mean of the two extreme terms, 8, 2, substituting 5, 5. This is the only irregularity in the scheme, and its motivation is musical; Bach seems to have wanted to separate out the word 'Kyrie', with its rising three-note figure, from the first words of the trope and was unwilling to prolong their note-values to make a four-bar unit, the smallest the scheme would allow. In view of the strength and consistency of the overall pattern we simply cannot refuse to make the adjustment which Bach certainly intended. In the following table, which shows the complete scheme, silent bars are shown in round brackets.

Kyrie I:	(4) 3 (4) 4 (3) 4 (3) 6 (4) 6
Christe:	(6) 4 (3) 3 (3) 3 (3) 4 (3) 3 (3) 4 (3) 6 (4) 6
Kyrie II:	(8) 2 (4) 4 (5) 5 (5) 4 (5) 6 (5) 6

The cantus firmus part of table Kyrie I is shown in Ex. 20, with the numerical relationships indicated.

Ex. 20. BWV 669 (cantus firmus).

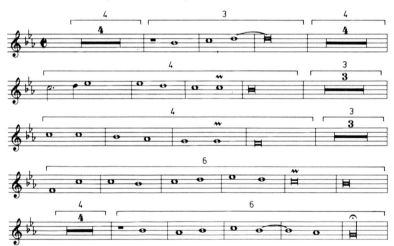

Secondly, the number of voices in the polyphony always gives the mean term of the progression it contains, as shown below.

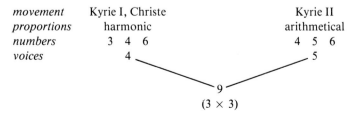

movement	Kyrie I, Christe	Kyrie II
proportions	harmonic	arithmetical
numbers	3 4 6	4 5 6
voices	4	5

9
(3 × 3)

The addition of the two means to make 9, which recalls several appearances of the addition $5 + 4 = 9$ in the fugue, calls for some comment. Three is the number of elements of which the mixture for the Platonic World-Soul is compounded (see Stage 1). In the Neoplatonist tradition the threefold division of the soul is identified with the faculties of reason (*logistikon*), emotion (*thymikon*) and appetite (*epithymetikon*).[25] In view of this tripartite division it is not surprising that throughout the Platonising Mass cycle Bach finds methods of emphasising the primacy of the number three and its square, nine, in ways which will be obvious to the reader.

Lesser Kyrie cycle (5 – 7). In these three short *manualiter* pieces, which are free contrapuntal workings of motifs derived from the Kyrie – Christe – Kyrie melodies, the esoteric significance is hidden in the time signatures, which employ an updated version of the mediaeval prolation system also found in the Gloria.[26] Bach's version of the system can be shown thus:

♩ – *modus* – ♩ – *tempus* – ♪ – *prolatio* – ♪

In the lesser Kyrie cycle, which employs the *modus* and *tempus* only, the division of the bar into *modus* and *tempus* relationships is as follows:

	t/s	♩ –	♩ –	♪	units per bar
Kyrie I	3/4	2	3		6
Christe	6/8	3	2		6
Kyrie II	9/8	3	3		9

This is the first introduction of the underlying principle of the third of the standard types of mensuration (geometric) to add to the other two types (arithmetical and harmonic) as expounded in the greater Kyrie cycle. Having begun with the harmonic division of the octave (3, 4, 6) and then continued with the arithmetical division of the resulting perfect 5th (4, 5, 6) Bach proceeds to proportion based, not on the mensuration of fixed integers, but on the division of a time unit into progressively smaller values, potentially infinite in number and governed by one type of relationship (sesquialtera proportion). The greater Kyrie cycle involves aggregation from a unit, the lesser with continuous division of a totality.

All the music in the number-music sections of the *Clavierübung* is related to the unvarying tactus. We have already observed the tactus-based proportional divisions in the fugue. The three movements of the greater Kyrie cycle (in ₵ time) also are apparently conceived in relation to the pulse tempo. That is, a strict application of the tactus-implied tempo (c. ♩ = 80) seems ideal for these movements, whereas any attempt to interpret (for example) the *alla breve* marking in the Prelude in the same way leads to disaster. The Mass preludes represent a faithful alignment of the *musica humana* of the human body with the *musica mundana* of the universe. In demonstrating the division of the unchanging tactus-related values of the durations, Bach was paying deliberate tribute to the vast corpus of writings on the Pythagorean theory of numbers, much of it not directly concerned with music. The Ars Nova movement itself has to be seen against the background of the work of thirteenth- and fourteenth-century mathematicians such as Jordanus Nemorarius, Gersonides and Nicholas Oresme, all of whom were concerned to the point of obsession with the theory of proportionality. Philippe de Vitry himself was a revered mathematician (Gersonides wrote *De numeris harmonicis* at de Vitry's request). [27]

Continuous proportions were one of the favourite topics of mediaeval mathematicians, who demonstrated how to form them by multiplication. The obvious methods, (whose relationship with the squaring and cubing of the Timaeus is clear) is to construct a pyramidal diagram of the type shown below. The two root numbers (here the imperfect 2 and the perfect 3) are written side by side and the successive stages produced by diagonal subdivision. Continuous proportion diagrams of this type were used by Boethius, by Jacob of Liège[28] and (though in ascending position) by one of the greatest of all mediaeval mathematicians, Nicholas Oresme.[29] Fig. 2 shows a continuous sesquialtera proportion diagram, with the numbers generated by Bach in the Gloria and lesser Kyrie cycles of the *Clavierübung* underlined.

$$\underline{2} \qquad \underline{3}$$

$$4 \qquad \underline{6} \qquad \underline{9}$$

$$\underline{8} \qquad \underline{12} \qquad \underline{18} \qquad 27$$

Fig. 2   Continuous sesquialtera proportions

Bach's musical microcosm is compounded of perfection and imperfection, combining multiples of the unstable, divided binary and the stable, unified ternary.

Gloria cycle (8 – 10). These are three contrasted preludes on the German metrical Gloria (*Allein Gott in der Höh' sei Ehr'*), the first and third *manualiter*, the second *pedaliter*. They will be referred to throughout as 'the Gloria cycle'. Here again, Bach employs his version of the prolation system, this time including all three tiers; *modus*, *tempus* and *prolatio*. The rhythmic relationships can be shown as follows:

t/s		𝅗𝅥	-	𝅘𝅥	-	𝅘𝅥𝅮	-	𝅘𝅥𝅮	*units per bar*
Gloria I	3/4 with sextolets			3		2		3	18
Gloria II	6/8 with semiquavers			2		3		2	12
Gloria III	4/4 with semiquavers			2		2		2	8

Here, however, the inner significance is numerical. The ratio of the three products (18, 12, 8) reduces to 9, 6, 4, which neatly relates geometric proportionality to Bach's treatment of the other types in the Kyrie cycle. Further, the stave-ruling of the three preludes 'underlines' the mean term (2, 3, 2), thus cementing the connection with the underlined harmonic and arithmetical means in the Kyrie.

Clavir Übung
bestehend in
Præludien, Allemanden, Couranten, Sarabanden, Giguen,
Menuetten, und andern Galanterien;
Denen Liebhabern zur Gemüths Ergoetzung verfertiget
von
Johann Sebastian Bach
Hochfürstl. Sächsisch-Weißenfelsischen würcklichen Capellmeistern
und
Directore Chori Musici Lipsiensis.
OPUS I.
In Verlegung des Autoris.
1731.

Plate I. Title-page of the original engraving of *Clavierübung* I British Library K 10 a 1 (reproduced by permission).

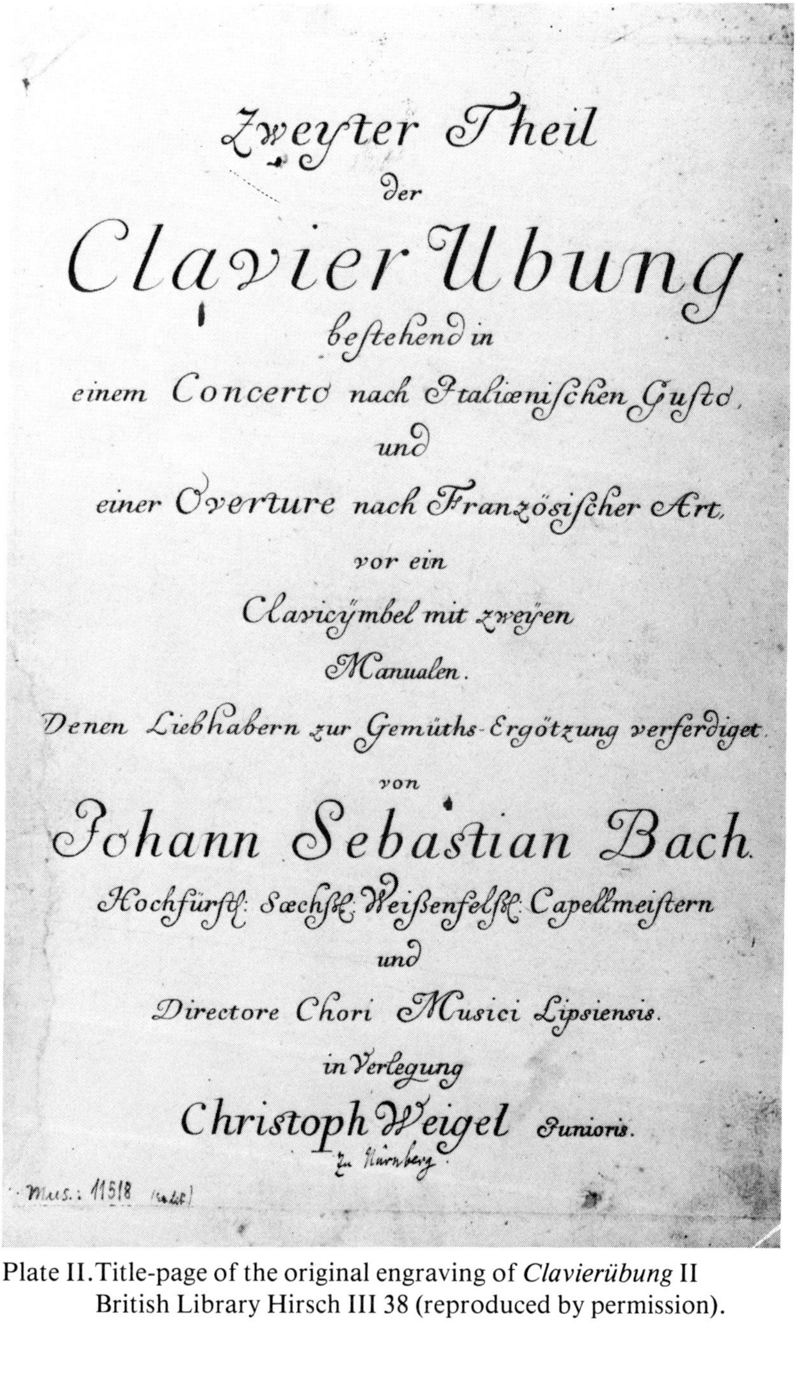

Zweyter Theil

der

Clavier Ubung

beſtehend in

einem Concerto nach Italiæniſchen Guſto,

und

einer Overture nach Franzöſiſcher Art,

vor ein

Clavicÿmbel mit zweÿen

Manualen.

Denen Liebhabern zur Gemüths-Ergötzung verferdiget

von

Johann Sebastian Bach.

Hochfürſtl: Sæchſß: Weißenfelſß: Capellmeiſtern

und

Directore Chori Musici Lipsiensis.

in Verlegung

Christoph Weigel Junioris.

zu Nürnberg.

Plate II. Title-page of the original engraving of *Clavierübung* II
British Library Hirsch III 38 (reproduced by permission).

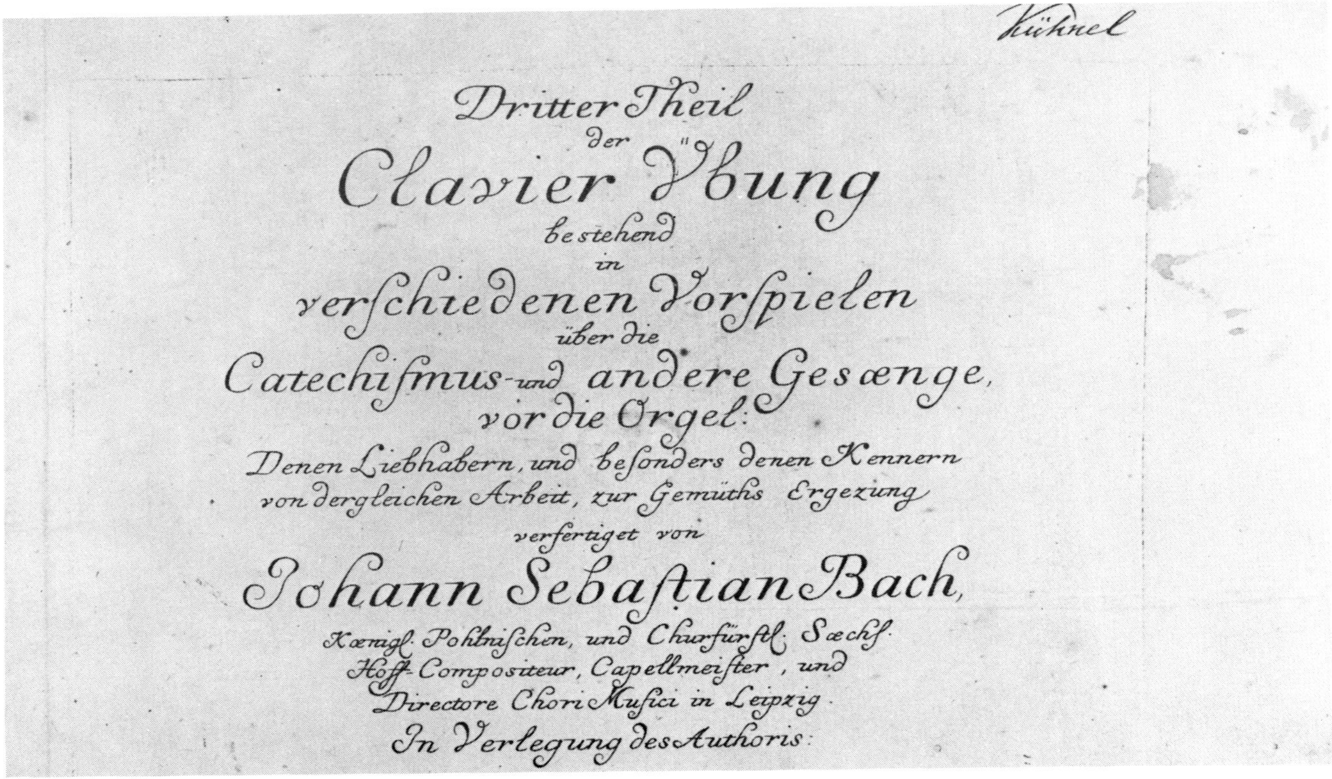

Titel

Dritter Theil
der
Clavier Übung
bestehend
in verschiedenen Vorspielen
über die
Catechismus- und andere Gesænge,
vor die Orgel:

Denen Liebhabern, und besonders denen Kennern
von dergleichen Arbeit, zur Gemüths Ergezung
verfertiget von

Johann Sebastian Bach,
Königl. Pohlnischen, und Churfürstl. Sæchs.
Hoff-Compositeur, Capellmeister, und
Directore Chori Musici in Leipzig.
In Verlegung des Authoris.

Plate III. Title-page of the original engraving of *Clavierübung III* British Library Hirsch III 39 (reproduced by permission).

Plate IV. Title-page of the original engraving of the Goldberg
Variations British Library Hirsch III 40 (reproduced by
permission).

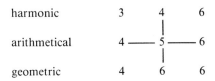

harmonic	3	4	6
arithmetical	4 ——	5 ——	6
geometric	4	6	6

The whole matrix could not be more systematically ordered. There are two fixed terms (4, 6) with the additional term first below, then between, then above them. However, the matrix has a deeper function, revealed in the central 'cross' of numbers (4, 5, 6) which gives the 'sounding numbers' of the major triad, known to the theory of Bach's day as *trias harmonica*.[30] The implicit harmonising of the three types of proportionality in the Gloria cycle, with the major triad occupying the central position, form a logical conclusion to Bach's developing exposition of proportionality in the three groups.

Tonal organisation. The creation of the elements of music is developed further in the tonal organisation of the Mass cycle as a whole, to which we now turn. It is designed to demonstrate the genesis and tuning of all the musical intervals. The three Gloria preludes are in F major, G major and A major respectively. The lesser Kyrie cycle is tonally unstable, the polyphony being permeated strongly by the Phrygian modality of the chant, but for the purposes of the esoteric structure, we have to take the E major chord on which all three constituent movements end (that is, the Phrygian final with *tierce de picardie*). In the absence of any other clearly defined tonal centre this seems an almost inevitable decision. At first sight a similar solution might seem appropriate for the greater Kyrie cycle also, since Kyrie I and Kyrie II both end with Phrygian cadences on G, reflecting the G-Phrygian modality of the chant. Here, however, another factor enters which has important consequences for the overall ordering of the set; the opening prelude can be paired not only with the fugue, but also with the greater Kyrie cycle.

The validity of this arrangement is confirmed by a mass (or Mass) of corroborative evidence. That it has a firm basis in the liturgical practice of Bach's day is shown by the well-known memorandum entered by Bach himself on the verso of the title-page of the autograph of Cantata 61 and headed *Anordnung des GottesDienstes in Leipzig am 1. Advent-Sontag frühe.*[31] The third item, 'Praeludieret auf das Kyrie, so gantz musicieret wird', indicates the usual practice in Leipzig; the sung Kyrie was preceded by an organ prelude.[32] Internal evidence establishes the pairing beyond question. Not only do we have the juxtaposition and the identity of key-signature, but also most of the oppositions already noted in the prelude-and-fugue pairing. First, there is the contrasting of galant and learned styles, which neatly accounts for the *stile antico* counterpoint employed throughout the Kyrie. Secondly, the opposition of verbal and numerical Trinity symbolism which is central to the prelude-fugue pairing can be read equally well into the prelude-Kyrie pairing; in the greater Kyrie cycle the three-term progressions, the three constituent movements and, most conspicuously, the Trinitarian Kyrie trope all invite this interpretation. The prelude and fugue have long been among the most popular items in the organist's repertoire; it would be pleasant if the equally valid 'prelude and Kyrie' could now join them.

The full implications of this pairing will be shown later. Our immediate concern is with its consequences for the tonality of the greater Kyrie cycle. On purely musical grounds this might be in doubt, since all three movements exhibit a number of sliding tonalities of which none could really be said to predominate. It is the pairing with the prelude which establishes that we are intended to take the main tonal centre from the three-flat key-signature and read it as E♭ major, a key which is indeed prominent, if not really pre-dominant, throughout all three movements. It is, indeed, the main tonality of the prelude-Kyrie unit.

The tonic (or final) triads for the three sub-cycles of the Mass cycle can now be shown. The triad itself has already been evolved from the 'triple Trinity' of proportions (Ex. 21).

Ex. 21.

The twofold significance of this progression is apparent from the bracketing. The three tonic triads of the Gloria cycle may be prefaced either by the E♭ major triad of the greater Kyrie cycle, producing a rising succession of three whole-tones, or by the E major triad of the lesser Kyrie cycle, giving a Dorian tetrachord. The two progressions are lettered A and B in Ex. 22.

Ex. 22.

This arrangement too has a liturgical as well as a musical logic behind it. It is equivalent to a view of the two Kyrie cycles as alternatives, as the indication 'alio modo' on Kyrie I of the lesser cycle implies, and of the whole Mass cycle as two constituent Kyrie-Gloria pairings.[33]

The B progression, which will be considered first, is our second encounter with the Dorian tetrachord. In the number music we are concerned, not with its ethical significance, but with its Pythagorean implications. The tetrachord was, as is well known, the method traditionally used by theorists to demonstrate the tuning of the intervals; rooted in Ptolemaeic music theory, it features in the works of Boethius, Jacob of Liège, Zarlino, Glareanus, Praetorius and a multitude of other standard writers. The tetrachord encompasses all musical intervals within the perfect fourth, and in computing values for them we are to employ the hallowed Pythagorean system which, like the Platonic cosmos, derives all its relationships from the root numbers 1, 2, 3. Their values, related to the notes of the tetrachord, are shown in Fig. 3.

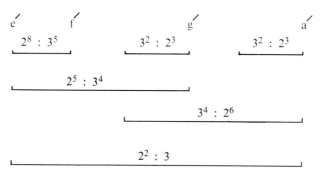

Fig. 3. *Intervallic Ratios Derived from Tetrachord*

This gives the following values for the smaller intervals.

semitone	256:243
tone	9:8
minor third	32:27
major third	81:64
perfect fourth	4:3

All the larger intervals can be dervied from these by harmonic inversion, except the tritone. This is neatly supplied by Ex. 22A, which shows its derivation from the Greater Tone (Fig. 4).

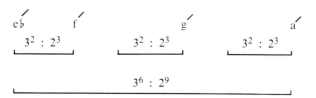

Fig. 4. *Derivation of Tritone*

The Pythagorean tritone thus acquires its value of 729:512.

Matter and spirit. Throughout the *musica arithmetica* sections, the number of voices in the polyphonic texture of each piece plays its part in the esoteric structure. In the greater Kyrie cycle, as we have seen, the number of voices supplies the mean term of the progression expressed by the bar ratios of the cantus

45

firmus. It now remains to examine the rest of the Mass cycle from this point of view.

All three movements of the shorter Kyrie cycle are à4, all three movements of the Gloria cycle à3. This introduces another Pythagorean commonplace: the equation of 3 with spirit and 4 with matter. The first is related to the Platonic threefold division of the soul, already noted, the second to all the traditional 'earthly' orders (elements, seasons, winds, directions). Their sum is the cosmic and mystic 7, as the number of planets our first reference to the remaining element of the quadrivium (astronomy). This 'mystic equation' can be read at a number of levels, either as spirit + matter = universe, or in later Christian elaborations as Trinity + Earth = Church, or trivium + quadrivium = liberal arts, or as the sum of cardinal and theological virtues. Two representative sources, both belonging to, or influenced by the Platonist tradition, are Augustine (*City of God* XI 31)[34] and Macrobius (*Commentary on the Dream of Scipio* I 6).[35] Macrobius, who according to Stahl based the relevant section of the *Commentary* on Porphyry's *Life of Pythagoras*,[36] was one of the most influential of all Neoplatonist writers. He devotes a considerable section to the number 7, and to the pairs of integers which can be added together to form it. Three, as 'the first to have a mean between two extremes to bind it together' is connected with the trinity of God – Mind – Soul to which Macrobius assigns the traditional function of two extremes and mean in his summary of this Neoplatonic doctrine in Ch. XIV. And, in Macrobius's own words:

> The number four is the first of all numbers to have two means. Borrowing the means from this number the Creator of the universe bound the elements together with an unbreakable chain, as was affirmed in Plato's Timaeus; in no other way could the elements earth and fire, so opposed and repugnant to each other, and spurning any communion of their natures, be mingled together and joined in so binding a union unless they were held together by the two means of earth and water.[37]

The reader may be referred to Stahl pp. 108 – 117 for Macrobius's detailed (and to modern reader somewhat bizarre) account of the number seven itself, except for the single remark that almost all of them related to the revelation of the unknown.

Matter and spirit, as twin attributes of the universe itself and of each created thing within it, are concepts essential to Bach's musical universe. One final significance for the numbers 3 and 4 is perhaps worth adding; both their sum (7) and their product (12) are concerned with the measurement of time, which, in the words of the *Timaeus*,

> came into being together with the Heaven, in order that, as they were brought into being together, so they may be dissolved together, if ever their dissolution should come to pass; and it is made after the pattern of the ever-enduring nature, in order that it may be as like that pattern as possible; for the pattern is a thing that has being for all eternity, whereas the Heaven has been and is and shall be perpetually throughout all Time.[38]

Numerology. The bar totals in the number-music element also contribute throughout to the grand design. We have already seen the role of the bar aggregates in the fugue (both overall and in the individual sections) in reinforcing the Trinity symbolism in which the piece is steeped. In the Mass preludes, however, Bach based his design on the individual numerals of the bar totals, which combine with the figures in the proportions to form an ingenious little number game which could perhaps be regarded as a kind of 'confirmer' for the reader's benefit.

If we count the bar totals of the three constituent cycles we arrive at the following totals

Greater Kyrie:	42 + 61 + 60	= 163
Lesser Kyrie:	32 + 30 + 34	= 96
Gloria:	48 + 126 + 20	= 194

If these totals are aligned with the proportion series generated in , the appropriate movements, their meaning immediately becomes clear.

	Bar total	Proportion series
Greater Kyrie:	⌈ 1 6 3	6 4 3
	⌊	6 5 4
Lesser Kyrie:	9 6	9 6
Gloria:	1 9 4	9 6 4

47

In each case the last two digits in the total supply the extreme terms of the series, while the number of digits mirrors the number of terms in the equivalent series.

By basing his number structures in the Mass preludes on the three classical proportions, Bach has modelled his musical microcosm on the three terrestrial or sublunary divisions of the quadrivium, expounded by Plato (*Republic* Book IV) and Boethius (*De institutione musica* Book I) and enshrined in the mediaeval system of the seven liberal arts. In the Catechism preludes, to which we now turn, he pursued a sharply contrasted ideal.

5 – Musica oratorica
(the Catechism Preludes)

With the twelve Catechism preludes (11 – 22) which, as we have already discovered, form a larger group of sixteen with the four Duetti, Bach returns to the rhetorical armoury of the word-music. To recapitulate, the twelve preludes are settings of the six Catechism chorales of Luther, set twice each and ranged according to the order of the main headings in the doctrinal section of the 'received' version of Luther's Lesser Catechism. Once again, in any consideration of the individual preludes it is essential not to lose sight of Bach's overall aim; in esoteric terms the preludes form part of Bach's (or Luther's) programme for the doctrinal instruction of the faithful. One consequence of this is that the rhetorical devices employed in the preludes are to be seen as communicated from master to pupil in a demonstrative sense, with the aim of instructing by giving pleasure. The didactic aim is aptly summed up by Sidney in his definition of poetry:

> Poetry therefore is an art of imitation, for so Aristotle termeth it in the word *Mimesis*, that is to say, a representing, counterfeiting, or figuring forth – to speak metaphorically, a speaking picture with this end, to teach and delight.[39]

Sidney's term 'speaking picture' puts in a nutshell the character of Bach's Catechism preludes, which 'figure forth' the pleasurable instruction meeted out to the young Lutheran neophyte by his master.

Naturally these preludes have been much discussed, and consequently few of the interpretations given here are advanced for the first time. Nevertheless, the realisation of the consistency with which Bach pursued his didactic aims, has led to two or three not uninteresting discoveries. In the discussion which follows the twelve preludes are taken in order, with Luther's important headings, already shown in Table 2, preceding the preludes to which they apply and lettered (*a*) – (*f*).

49

(a) Die zehn Gebote, wie sie ein   The ten commandments: how the
Hausvater seinem Gesinde   master of the house should
einfältiglich vorhalten soll   expound them in a simple manner
to his household

Dies sind die heil'gen zehn Gebot' I (11). Headed 'a 2 Clav. et
Ped. Canto fermo in Canone' this prelude has the chorale in a free
octave canon, with the lines widely separated. The nature of the
accompanying free material is best illustrated by a quotation
(Ex. 23).

Ex. 23. BWV 678, bars 1 – 7.

For the opening, Dietrich's interpretation[40] seems so obviously
correct that its failure to win general acceptance is little short of
amazing. The passage, with its drone bass and placid diatonic

melody reinforcing the 6/4 time-signature, is in the manner of the *piffaro*. An example for comparison is readily available in the Pastorale BWV 590 (Ex. 24).

Ex. 24. BWV 590, bars 1 – 4.

The *piffaro* is followed by cheerful major arpeggios, portraying joy (bar 4). But then comes an abrupt change of character, produced by the figures for sighs (bar 5) and trickling tears (bar 6), the former accompanied by the 'grief' figure (the descending chromatic tetrachord) in the alto voice. Last of all comes the chorale melody itself, bringing to mind the opening words '*these are the holy Ten Commandments*' and given in canon (*canon =* law). The effect on the accompanying voices is immediate; the 'joy' figure returns (bars 8 – 9) and the chromatic sighs of bar 6 are transformed into a more cheerful diatonic form (bar 9). The programme could hardly be more clearly outlined; the 'speaking picture' represents, in terms rooted in the Pauline epistles, the Age of Nature, the Fall of Man, and the gift of the Law of Moses. For a summary of other interpretations, here and throughout the Catechism cycle, the reader is referred to Williams pp. 201 – 225.

Dies sind die heil'gen zehn Gebot' II (12). There are ten entries of the fughetta subject, as many writers have pointed out. This device should in no way be confused with the number symbolism of the Mass cycle; it is a gestural device. The ten commandments are, as it were, counted out by the master's pointing finger.

A second layer of meaning has been discovered by Leaver[41] who has illuminated the significance of the gigue rhythm which pervades the prelude. This is apparent from the iambic lilt of the subject (Ex. 25)

Ex. 25. BWV 679, bars 1 – 3.

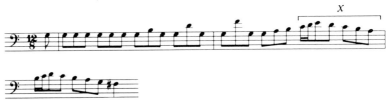

and from the characteristic fingerprint (figure *x*) which may be compared with another example from the C major cello suite BWV 1009 (Ex. 26).

Ex. 26. BWV 1009, Gigue, bars 93 – 100

As Leaver points out, Bach's use of gigue rhythm (and, one might add, of the 'complaisant' 12/8 metre from Duetto III) expresses the cheerful obedience demanded of the pupil and exhorted by Luther in the closing words of the relevant section of the Lesser Catechism: 'we should ... gladly (*gerne*) obey his commandments'. This is no mere *jeu d'esprit*, but a Protestant insistence on the insufficiency of works for salvation. As such it may perhaps be seen as pointing towards the next chorale, which introduces the concept of justification by faith.

(b)	Der Glaube, wie ein Haus-vater denselbigen seinem Gesinde aufs einfältigste vorhalten soll	The Creed: how the master of the house should expound it in the simplest manner to his household

Wir glauben all' an einen Gott I (13). The three upper voices (manual) play an extended fugue on the first line of the melody, thus implicitly making the avowal of its text: 'we all believe in one God'. This much is simple, but a new interpretation is offered here for the independent pedal figure (Ex. 27) which appears six times widely spaced out by rests.

Ex. 27. BWV 680 bars 4 – 9.

This familiar figure, comprising a rising and falling octave, consists of two elements, both of which have the common characteristic of 'linked' intervals (rising fourths in the first element, falling thirds in the second). This is the basis for its interpretation as the figure for a chain. That this interpretation can be supported from previous music nourished by humanist thought can be shown from Byrd's motet *Solve iubente Deo* (*Gradualia*, 1607) quoted in Ex. 28.

Ex. 28. Byrd, *Solve iubente Deo* (1607) bars 19 – 22.

TER - RA - RUM, PE - TRE, CA - TE - NAS, CA - TE -

NAS, CA - TE - NAS

There are altogether thirteen entries of the *échappée* figure applied to the word *catenas*. An excellent example of Bach's use of it with the same meaning occurs in the *Orgelbüchlein* prelude on *Christ lag in Todesbanden* (BWV 625) in which the *échappée* figure, accompanying the chorale, represents the fetters of death (Ex. 29).

Ex. 29. BWV 625, bars 1 – 4.

In the *Clavierübung* prelude on *Wir glauben all'* the chain figure 'anchors' the first note of the fugue (D) to its lower octave on both its first and last appearances. In biblical terms this hardly needs explanation; the three manual voices are, in Pauline language, 'grounded and steadfast' in faith (*Colossians* 1,23). More concretely, it may be a reference to the Christian symbolism of the anchor (see *Hebrews* 6,19). The chain image reappears, this time in visual aspect, in the syncopated form taken by the subject. The rhythm

is related to fourth-species counterpoint, referred to as *ligatura* or *syncopatio* by Fux (1725) and *ligature* by Mozart; its most famous musical derivative is the *ligature e durezze* style of the seventeenth-century Italian organists. Bach himself used the term *per syncopationes et per ligaturas* to describe it in the tenth of the Fourteen Canons BWV 1087. In *Wir glauben all'* the tie (*ligatura*) is the chain binding the syncopated first note of the chorale to the bar-line.

Wir glauben all' an einen Gott II (14). In this miniature French overture the regal dotted rhythms once again symbolise the majesty of God the Father. The reader is referred to the comments on the prelude (p. 20).

(c)	Das Vaterunser, wie ein Hausvater dasselbige seinem Gesinde aufs einfältigste vorhalten soll	The Lord's Prayer: how the master of the house should expound it in the simplest manner to his household

Vater unser im Himmelreich I (15). Here again the chorale melody is given out in octave canon (*Canto fermo in Canone*) which on this occasion probably suggests nothing more than the plural form of the first line (that is, two petitioners). Around this structural framework two further voices weave a dialogue in which is unmistakably the pathetic, affective manner of the instrumental *arioso* or *adagio*. There are no tempo markings in the *Clavierübung*, but in this movement the short note-values, the rich detail and the wealth of articulation marks establish the prelude beyond doubt as a slow movement (Ex. 30).

Ex. 30. BWV 682, bars 1 – 7.

continued

This could perfectly well be the opening of a trio-sonata; in fact the bass, written in terms of a gamba or continuo cello, is not easy to play on organ pedals. On the performance of such movements, Quantz has the following observation:

> To play an Adagio well, you must enter as much as possible into a calm and almost melancholy mood, so that you execute what you have to play in the same state of mind as that in which the composer wrote it. A true Adagio must resemble a flattering petition. For just as anyone who wishes to request something from a person to whom he owes particular respect will scarcely achieve his object with bold and impudent threats, so here you will scarcely engage, soften, and touch your listener with a bold and bizarre manner of playing. For that which does not come from the heart does not easily reach the heart.[42]

These famous remarks put in a nutshell the *Affekt* of Bach's prelude; with its staccato semiquaver triplets and persistent Lombard rhythms it represents, in Quantz's language, 'a melancholy and pathetic Adagio' of a distinctly galant stamp. The 'flattering petition', addressed to God the Father by the implied text of the Lord's Prayer, is based on a subject which decorously 'colours' the first line of the tune.

Vater unser im Himmelreich II (16). The interpretation of this *manualiter* prelude presents no difficulties. The melody, this time stated straight through, is accompanied by the rushing ascending and descending scales associated elsewhere in Bach's music with angels, treated as emissaries between God and man. The figure is prominent in the two preludes on *Vom Himmel hoch* (BWV 701, 738) and in the last of the Canonic Variations on the same chorale

(BWV 769) where its significance needs no elaboration. In the present case the 'speaking picture' shows God the Father 'in Heaven' surrounded by the angelic host.

(d) Das Sakrament der heiligen Taufe, wie dasselbige ein Hausvater seinem Gesinde soll einfältig vorhalten

The sacrament of Holy Baptism: how the master of the house should expound it in a simple manner to his household

Christ unser Herr zum Jordan kam I (17). The chorale is given out in the pedal, the lines separated (as usual in the *pedaliter* settings) by rests. The accompanying material consists of the baroque cross theme (RH) and running semiquavers (LH) portraying Christ and the Jordan. An additional point, which the present writer has not seen elsewhere, concerns the first pedal entry. When the pedal gives out the first line (corresponding to the words of the title) the wave figure momentarily rises above the cross theme (this occurs nowhere else in the prelude) as Christ's body is dipped into the Jordan (Ex. 31).

Ex. 31. BWV 684, bars 6 – 9.

Christ unser Herr zum Jordan kam II (18). In the *manualiter* setting the first line of the chorale melody is treated as a fugue by inversion, each entry being combined with another form of the wave figure as countersubject. It is worth noting that the wave figure accompanies the notes corresponding to 'zum Jordan kam', the 'Christ unser Herr' portion appearing alone (Ex. 32).

Ex. 32. BWV 685, bars 1 – 3.

The fugue has no episodes, comprising six successive entries of subject and countersubject (odd-numbered entries direct, even-numbered entries inverted). As Keller has pointed out,[43] the reference is undoubtedly to the threefold immersion in baptism, with 'Christ our Lord' (the chorale) three times inverted, as through the agency of the wave figure.

(e)	Wie man die Einfältigen soll lehren beichten	How to teach the simple to make confession

Aus teifer Not schrei' ich zu dir I (19). This extraordinary piece, which marks the only intrusion of the *stile antico* into the *oratorica* section of the *Clavierübung*, is an organ motet à6 (four manual and two pedal voices) with the cantus firmus in the tenor (the upper pedal voice). This archaic texture, unique in Bach's organ music, has been traced back to two pieces in Scheidt's *Tabulatura nova* (1624); in general, the style and construction look back further to the sixteenth-century tradition of polyphonic chorale settings and *Tenorlieder*. It is perhaps worth quoting an example of the latter published in 1544[44] and treating the same melody; with its booming tenor melody and conscientiously worked prefatory imitations it is connected to the Bach prelude by a tradition spanning two centures (Ex. 33).

Ex. 33. Resinarius, *Aus tiefer Not* (1544) bars 1 – 13

Of course, the reference back to the vocal model provides the clue to the rhetorical significance of the music. The polyphonic voices become human petitioners, whose clamorous appeals (echoing the text of the chorale) are accentuated by the arching lines and reiterated *plorans semitonus* of the melody (no doubt this was what prompted Bach's choice of this particular chorale for motet treatment).

Aus tiefer Not schrei' ich zu dir II (20). In the *manualiter* setting a somewhat similar technique is used, though with a different end in view. The chorale melody, stated in minims with the lines spaced out by rests, is in the soprano, with the accompanying texture saturated with imitations of the line concerned. Here imitations are all-pervasive (in the *pedaliter* prelude they are mainly prefatory). The two most important differences of approach, however, are the lack of the strong choral background and (related to this) the equal prominence of direct and inverted entries, which form a maze of contrapuntal activity throughout the main entries in the uppermost voice. These direct and inverted entries in double diminution form the rhetorical component, portraying the 'distress' of the first line. Another use of a jumble of rising and falling entries with this meaning occurs in the *Orgelbüchlein* prelude on *Wenn wir in höchsten Nöthen sein* (BWV 641) and (more strongly emphasised) in the reworking of the same prelude to form the so-called *Sterbchoral* (BWV 668).

(f)	Das Sakrament des Altars, wie ein Hausvater dasselbige seinem Gesinde einfaltiglich vorhalten soll	The Eucharist: how the master of the house should expound it in the simplest manner to his household

Jesus Christus unser Heiland I (21). The two preludes on *Jesus Christus unser Heiland* seem to represent cases where the point has most conspicuously been missed. The *pedaliter* setting has the melody as a pedal cantus firmus, with the lines exceptionally widely spaced. Meanwhile two manual voices carry on a vigorous fugal dialogue on the following subject (Ex. 34):

Ex. 34. BWV 688, bars 1 – 6.

This has been subjected to all manner of bizarre interpretations, but Bach himself provided a clue which seems to have remained unrecognised; of a total of 21 chorale preludes contained in the *Clavierübung* this is the only one which Bach labelled, not with the first line of the text, but with the first two lines. The title as given by Bach reads, 'Jesus Christus, unser Heiland, der von uns den Zorn Gottes wandt'. There is an external, practical reason for this; Bach wished to distinguish the chorale from another beginning *Jesus Christus unser Heiland / der den Tod überwand.* However, even this purely pragmatic distinction Bach managed to make functional in the light of the esoteric structure. It is worth pointing out that: in all twelve Catechism preludes the meaning of the central figure can be derived from the title *as given by Bach.* The first four bars of the prelude consist of pairs of converging lines which spring apart again at the opening of each bar, rather as though the bar-line itself was acting as a buffer to their progress; the figure might be represented thus (Fig. 5):

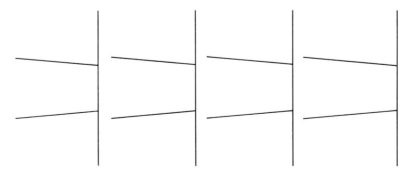

Fig. 5.   Graphic interpretation of the subject of BWV 688

61

Quite simply, the wrath of God descends to meet Man, but is turned aside by the atonement of Christ 'who turned the wrath of God from us'. The other dominating melodic figure of the piece, which appears for the first time in bar 6, is the falling group of semiquavers which forms the *perpetuum* mobile background to much of the prelude. These flowing semiquavers, which have a pronounced tendency to fall in groups of four, represent the falling of drops of blood (conceived, of course, in a doctrinal sense as the redeeming blood of Christ).

Jesus Christus unser Heiland II (22). The *manualiter* setting is the last of the twelve Catechism preludes, and from the present viewpoint the most intriguing. Each of the first eleven preludes is connected to its title by a verbal image or rhetorical programme by which the music is securely tied to Luther's directions, and, more broadly, to the ideals of the *oratorica* group as a whole. Here there is no such connection. We appear to be dealing with a completely abstract conception, related to the chorale only by its use of the first line of the tune. Yet the position of the prelude within the Catechism group gives the clearest possible signal (as Bach intended that it should) that we are to look for a significance which gives it a figural role to play. The pattern created by eleven chorale preludes (and the four Duetti), and the consequent expectation raised in the reader's mind, impel him towards the discovery of the boldest and most surprising device in the whole of the group.

The prelude takes the form of an extended four-part fugue on the first line of the melody. Yet it is far from the character of the 'normal' mature Bach fugue. Almost the central characteristic of Bach's fugal style is the working together of tonal, thematic and textural elements to produce a massive, controlled sense of architecture; it is the apparently effortless union of structure and organic growth, realised through fugal technique, which accounts for the traditional view of the fugue as the form in which Bach was most essentially himself. It is precisely these qualities of organic growth and architecture which are absent in the *manualiter* prelude on *Jesus Christus*. Tonally, there are no major structural modulations away from the tonic. The most important cadences outside the tonic are in the dominant minor (C minor, bar 19), the subdominant minor (B♭ minor, bar 36) and again the dominant minor (C minor, bar 44). Of these the first two are followed rapidly by returns to the tonic, while the third gives rise to a short sequential episode (even this is short-lived). Apart from a handful of kaleidoscopic sequential modulations of no structural import the whole fugue is firmly rooted in the tonic. The overall effect of this is to heighten the sense (reinforced by other methods) of a free, unbounded, extensile form in which tonal architecture plays no defining role.

Thematically and structurally, the whole movement is quite exceptionally loosely knit. Of the major episodes, none as much as hints at the chorale itself; all of them are based on the inconsequential subsidiary figures quoted in Ex. 35 (a – d).

Ex. 35. BWV 689.

(a)

(b) (= (a) inverted)

(c)

(d)

The loose-limbed feel of the movement is apparent from as early as bars 5 – 6, when a non-developing codetta deliberately loosens the joints of the exposition. In general, the succession of entries seems almost haphazard, dropping casually into the meandering current of the episodes. Perhaps there is no more striking illustration of the character of the fugue than its ending, with its spun-out final cadence (Ex. 36).

Ex. 36. BWV 689, bars 57 – end.

The character of the fugue can be simply defined; it is written-out improvisation. There is, of course, one familiar example of a mature Bach improvisation for comparison: the Ricercare à3 from the Musical Offering. Here Bach's use of elaborate humanistic figures suggests that the written-out version may be one degree removed from the fugue improvised to Frederick the Great at Potsdam, but the basis in improvisation is strong enough for the same features to be recognisable. The loose, free construction, the diffuseness, the abundance of non-thematic ideas which enter and drop out unexpectedly, have all been noted by Bach commentators.

The view of *Jesus Christus* as written-out improvisation gives the clue to its function. For *Jesus Christus unser Heiland* was (and remains) the most famous of all Lutheran Communion hymns, the standard poetic expression of Lutheran sacramental doctrine and as such undoubtedly a regular feature of Communion in Bach's Leipzig. Apart from the two preludes on the *Clavierübung*, Bach composed two other large-scale chorale preludes on it (BWV 665, 666) and a harmonisation of the tune (Riemenschneider 30). For a description of the exact course of events during the administration of the sacraments in the Leipzig churches we can do no better than Bach's above-mentioned autograph memorandum (see p. 43), in which item 14 reads as follows:

Praelud. auf die *Music.* Und nach selbiger wechselsweise *praelud.* v *Choräle* gesungen, biß die *Communion* zu Ende & sic porrò.[45]	Preluding on the composition, After the same, alternate preluding and singing of chorales until the end of the Communion, and so on.

What 'die Music' consisted of is not entirely clear,[46] but the second part of the entry gives the setting for *Jesus Christus*; it can surely be nothing other than a *präludiert* chorale fugue of the type improvised by Bach *sub communione* and designed to precede the singing of the chorale itself. As a unique example of a written-out communion improvisation by Bach it is a precious document, but here it is only necessary to point out its symbolic function; it is nothing less than a dramatic or scenic evocation of Communion in the Leipzig churches. Though Bach did not occupy the organist's post there, he continued to enjoy legendary fame as an organist throughout the second half of his career, and the point would have been more easily appreciated by the early purchasers of the set who were not called upon to reconstruct Bach's improvisation technique at a distance of two centuries.

Tonal organisation. It has been generally recognised that most of the twelve Catechism preludes have modal key-signatures (in fact it was first pointed out by Kirnberger in 1776), but the significance of this has been missed. To appreciate the unified scheme formed by the twelve key-centres it is necessary to re-transpose the transposed finals back to their original position within the Glareanus twelve-mode system as shown in Table 4. With the reordering of the finals, the series of triads forms a rising and falling cycle of fifths (Ex. 37).

Table 4.   The tonal organisation of the Catechism Preludes

Title	Implied mode	Retransposed final
Dies sind die heil'gen zehn Gebot' I	G-Mixolydian	G
Dies sind die heil'gen zehn Gebot' II	G-Mixolydian	G
Wir glauben all' an einen Gott I	D-Dorian	D
Wir glauben all' an einen Gott II	E-Dorian	D
Vater unser im Himmelreich I	E-Dorian	D
Vater unser im Himmelreich II	D-Dorian	D
Christ unser Herr zum Jordan kam I	G-Aeolian	A
Christ unser Herr zum Jordan kam II	A-Aeolian	A
Aus tiefer Not schrei' ich zu dir I	E-Phrygian	E
Aus tiefer Not schrei' ich zu dir II	F♯-Phrygian	E
Jesus Christus unser Heiland I	D-Aeolian	A
Jesus Christus unser Heiland II	F-Dorian	D

Ex. 37.

This will be recognised as a traditional illustration of the evil consequences of trying to combine the Pythagorean tuning system
with the diatonic scale. The roots and fifths of the triads outline
the 'opened-out' pentatonic scale G-D-A-E-B, but one further
movement in the same direction produces the *diabolus in musica*
B-F (of course, the 'white-note' tonal field defined by the thirds
of the triads prevents us from substituting F♯ for F). Therefore
the triads progress no further, but return downwards. The shun-
ning of the devil, as the esoteric principle behind the tonal
organisation of the Catechism cycle, is entirely appropriate to the
aims of Luther, whose consciousness of a diabolical presence
appears to have been more than usually vivid. The text of the

66

Catechism is full of ringing denunciations of those who fail to comply, branding them as children of the Devil. Also worthy of note is Luther's gloss on the clause 'and lead us not into temptation' in the Lord's Prayer:

> Indeed, God does not tempt anyone, but in this prayer we ask that God will keep and preserve us, and that the Devil, the world and our flesh do not betray and seduce us into error, despair and other great sins and blasphemies, and that though we were hard pressed thereby, we shall yet conquer and gain victory.[47]

Numerical grouping. It will long have been apparent that the total numbers of movements in the Mass cycle (9) and the Vesper cycle (16) are, as the squares on 3 and 4, an expression of the matter-spirit dualism also noted in the polyphonic texture of the lesser Kyrie and Gloria cycles. The 3×3 grouping in the Mass cycle is obvious. To articulate the 4×4 grouping within the Vesper cycle Bach uses the stave-ruling. The Duetti, forming one of the four groups, are of course engraved on two staves, but the first in each group of four Vesper preludes is engraved on three staves, the other three on two. The result of this arrangement might be shows as

$$\underline{|3\ 2\ 2\ 2|3\ 2\ 2\ 2|3\ 2\ 2\ 2|\text{Duetti}|}$$

I	II	III	IV

This final element completes the analysis of the antithesis of ideas which lies at the heart of the esoteric structure. At the risk of over-simplifying Bach's rich, complex presentation of the opposition of ideas in the two central cycles, we shall conclude this section with a summary list of the dualities (some traditional, some Bachian elaborations) which are either stated or implied in the two cycles (Table 5).

Table 5. Opposed concepts in the esoteric structure

Musica arithmetica	Musica oratorica
3	4
spirit	matter
odd	even
active	passive
male	female
light	dark
fire	water
Heaven	Earth
Pythagoras	Luther
Pagan	Christian
ancient	modern
Graeco-Roman	Germanic
Mass	Vespers
Universe	Man
number/geometry	word
symbol	figure
fugue	prelude
stile antico	style galant
Italy	France
choir	orchestra

6 – The Central Design

The central design, which draws together all the elements so far considered into a unified whole, embraces number and tonal organisation. Its most important constituent, however, is the mandala-like geometric microcosm which is to be constructed by a process of logical and elegant simplicity involving already established relationships among the various inner cycles. In this section the various planes of the central design will be described in turn.

Geometric microcosm. It has already been asserted that the fourfold division of the contents of the *Clavierübung* represents a cycle of religious observance for a Lutheran Sunday: morning blessing, Mass, Vespers, evening blessing. There can be no doubt as to the geometric equivalent for this order; placing the fourfold order of religious exercise within the unending succession of daily revolutions of the Earth produces the time-honoured expression of the finite (earthly) order within the infinite (heavenly): the square within the circle (Fig. 6).

From this viewpoint we can again take up Luther's instructions for morning and evening prayer, which are associated respectively with the opening prelude and the closing fugue.

Des Morgens, so du aus dem Bette fährest, sollst du dich segnen mit dem heiligen Kreuz . . .	In the morning, when you get up, you are to bless yourself with the Holy Cross . . .
Des Abends, wenn du zu Bette gehest, sollst du dich segnen mit dem heiligen Kreuz . . . [48]	In the evening, when you go to bed, you are to bless yourself with the Holy Cross . . .

The consequences of following this instruction are shown in Fig. 7. By making the connection prelude – Vespers and Mass – fugue the cross joins opposite poles of the word – music and number – music groups, creating an intersection between them at the centre. It also provides the final confirmation of the

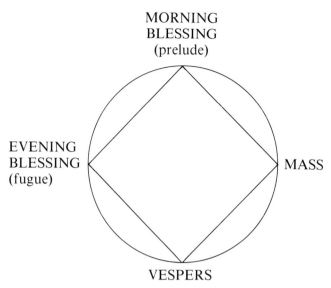

Fig. 6.   The fourfold order

correctness of the geometrical construction, and of our association of prelude and fugue with Luther's morning and evening
blessing.

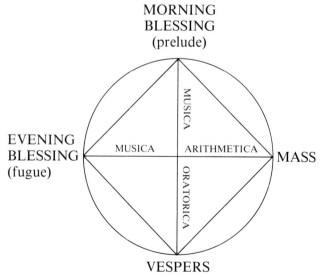

Fig. 7.   The sign of the cross

70

The next step concerns the prelude and fugue. It is obvious that if the cycle is 'lived' in a forward direction the prelude and fugue are in the wrong order. Yet the validity of the pairing, of which the fourfold order fails to take account, is beyond question. The only way to unify the prelude and fugue from the arrangement shown in Fig. 6 is to traverse the cycle in an anti-clockwise direction: that is, *to adopt reverse time*.

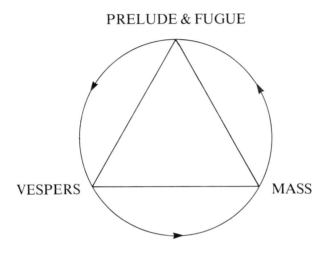

Fig. 8.   The reverse time cycle

The result, shown in Fig. 8, is the disappearance of the fourfold order; the ordering is now threefold (triangular). One difference of principle between the fourfold order (Fig. 6) and the threefold order (Fig. 8) should be noted; whereas the position of the square is fixed by the need to keep the cross in an orthagonal position, the triangle can be freely rotated. The prelude and fugue, which now form a unity, are no longer bound to the geometric discipline created by Luther's two instructions.

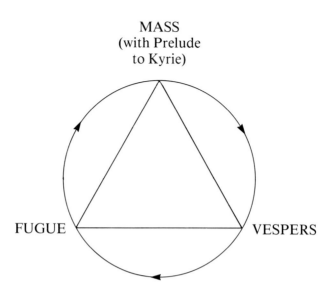

Fig. 9. The forward time cycle

We next examine the consequences of 'living' the cycle forwards (Fig. 9). Here the already established pairing of prelude and greater Kyrie cycle comes into its own, once more reducing the fourfold cycle to a threefold (triangular) cycle. Here again, the triangle can be freely rotated since the matutinal and vesperal connections of prelude and fugue have been severed.

This raises an interesting question. If traversing the cycle in either forward or reverse form transforms the fourfold order into a threefold order, in what sense could the former be said to exist at all? There can be only one answer: from the Eternal Present. The ideal ordering shown in Fig. 6, embracing both directional movements, is eternally manifest, thus fulfilling one of the traditional objects of the mandala, to facilitate the mental habit of thinking outside Time. The three cycles, then, represent forward time, reverse time and eternity.

We can now assemble the complete geometric microcosm. The correct position for the two triangles cannot be doubted; placed in opposed positions they form yet another religious symbol: the hexagram (Fig.10).

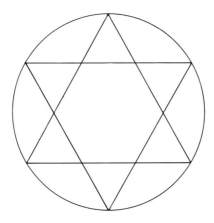

Fig. 10. Hexagram and circle

The completed microcosm, shown in Fig. 11, is made up of three superimposed planes, representing the forward, reverse and eternal orders. It can truly be said to be the final consummation of the esoteric structure, the goal to which Bach has led his readers step by step through the maze of devices employed

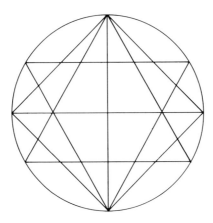

Fig. 11. The geometric microcosm

throughout the constituent cycles and individual pieces. The geometric microcosm, used as an object for religious contemplation, is a form known from a wide variety of manifestations in religious art. They range from the Eastern mandala and the decorative patterns of Islamic art to the polygon-within-circle groundplans of the round churches of the Templars and the circular plans also adopted in Alberti's *De re aedificatoria* (1443 – 52) and put into practice widely in the ecclesiastical architecture of the following century.[49] Robin Headlam Wells has recently produced a study of microcosmic geometry in the Renaissance lute rose, in which the square and hexagram are the predominant internal forms.[50] Its most brilliant manifestations in Western art are found in the rose windows of the French cathedrals, which are products of the same tradition of learning which produced Bach's esoteric structure. Their manifest and hidden geometry, encompassing bewilderingly complex developments of the square-within-circle motif, pentagrams, dodecagrams and Fibonacci series, has been discussed at length in a study by Cowen.[51]

In this (by no means exhaustive) summary of some possible readings of Bach's design it is necessary to bear in mind that the ideas never spring from nowhere, but have already been 'planted' by Bach at some previous stage in the unfolding of the esoteric structure. The two triangles forming the hexagram are associated in Bach's scheme with forward and reverse time respectively; their conjunction, which appears from six points of view, represents the meeting of past and future (the loop in time). This introduces, by transference, the traditional symbolism of the hexagram, the conjunction of opposites (fire – water, male – female) and hence the divine act of creation (it does in fact link opposed corners of the square). The hexagram has six points (six, as the sum of its own factors, is the first perfect number), and as a six-pointed star it symbolises the illumination which has led the reader through the labyrinthine paths of the inner structure.

As we have seen, the cross connects opposite poles of the 'human' and 'universal' elements of the structure, and with them all the layers of meaning accumulated throughout the Mass and Catechism-Duetti groups. The two arms, richly imbued with the meanings summarised in Table 5 (p. 68) intersect at the centre,

74

representing the Deity. The cross is also a fourfold radiation from the centre, showing the corners of the square (representing the fourfold orders of elements, seasons, winds, directions and humours) emanating from the Creator God and returning by the fourfold path to the sacred centre. The circle (or triple circle), which touches and embraces all the other designs, has (apart from Bach's explicit significations of forward time, reverse time and eternity) its traditional meanings (love, perfection, infinity and all the temporal and celestial cycles). Lastly, it has to be remembered that the whole design, depicted here as a static figure in plane geometry, is the summation of a series of moving cycles whose courses are defined by the constituent figures. These patterns, and the multitude of more complex patterns produced by meetings at the 25 intersections, form the choreography of the cosmic dance into which all the elements of Bach's musical microcosm are drawn. Bach and the Dance of God; Wilfred Mellers' title, used for a highly penetrative general study of Bach's music, could hardly be more apt here.

Tonal organisation. The tonal organisation of the individual groupings has already been discussed. Ex. 38 shows the integrated tonal scheme of the entire set.

Ex. 38.

This requires little comment. The only points so far unexplored are the ligatures between the internal cycles, which are apparent from the example. First, the G major triad which opens the Catechism cycle is also the 'mean term' of the ascending progression in the Gloria cycle: secondly, the final D minor triad of the Catechism cycle extends the scale progression of the Duetti: thirdly, the final A minor triad of the Duetti is tonally in an opposed position to the E♭ major triad of the fugue, thus extending the cyclic form of the *Clavierübung* to the tonal plane. In accordance with the reversibility of the cycle, the whole progression can be read either forwards or backwards. The overall tonal organisation also explains one more factor in the organisation of the individual cycles – the appearance of the Dorian tetrachord expressed first in major, then in 'white note' triads. In each case, as can be seen from the example, the discrepancy can be explained by the need to connect them satisfactorily with chords drawn from other cycles.

The numerical signature. The derivation of the Bach and J.S. Bach gematria, which adds a delightful final touch to the esoteric structure, is shown in Table 6. Bach's interest in the number 14, as the gematria of his own surname, is by now well known; it is manifest, for example in the fourteen canons which Bach added as a manuscript appendage to his own copy of the Goldberg Variations, in his eight-year wait to become the fourteenth member of Mizler's *Societät der musikalischen Wissenschaften* and in the famous Haussmann portrait of 1746. In this portrait, which was submitted as a condition of membership of the society, the canon Bach holds in his hand has fourteen notes in the two upper voices, and Bach's coat has fourteen silver buttons. The fact that the canon in the Haussmann portrait is one of the fourteen from the MS additions to the Goldberg variations creates a link between all these manifestations and the Mizler society which will later be found of importance. And, as Gregory Butler has recently discovered,[52] the quadruple fugue in *Die Kunst der Fuge*, incorporating the BACH theme, was intended by Bach as Contrapunctus 14, forming a musical signature to the cycle. A large number of speculations drawn from bar numbers, note-counting, stave-ruling and the like will be found in the more recent Bach literature. The appearance of the addition sum $14 + 27 = 41$ provides a striking confirmation of a theory first proposed by Smend,[53] who pointed out that in the cantus firmus voice of the *Sterbchoral* (*Wenn wir in höchsten Nöthen sein*, BWV 668) there are 41 notes, 14 for the first line of the tune and

27 for the last three. And a second example brings us back home; *Clavierübung* I contains a total of 41 movements, *Clavierübung* II 14, and *Clavierübung* III 27.

Table 6.   Bach's numerical signature

$27(3^3)$ = 1 + 9 + 16 + 1

Since 1 is not a number, take 9 and 16.

9 = 3 × 3
16 = 4 × 4

spirit + matter = universe

3	3
4	4
7	7

7 + 7 = 14

also   2 + 1 + 3 + 8 = 14

gematria B   A   C   H

27 + 14 = 41

also   9 + 18 + 14 = 41

gematria   J   S   BACH

NB: In old script I and J are identical, therefore I = 9, J = 9, K = 10 etc.

7 – The Purpose of the Esoteric Structure

Certain features of the wording of the title-page can now be recognised as clues warning the reader of the existence of the esoteric structure. To grasp their meaning it is necessary to compare in detail the wording of the title-page of all four *Clavierübung* collections. They are accordingly reproduced as Plates I – IV (pp. 38 – 41).

We begin with the four headings, which are as follows:

I		Clavir Ubung
II	Zweyter Theil der	Clavier Ubung
III	Dritter Theil der	Clavier Ubung
IV		Clavier Ubung

In *Clavierübung* III the first word to strike the eye of the reader is the ordinal *Dritter*, the number 3 (together with its square and cube) being the predominating figure in the esoteric structure. Similarly, in *Clavierübung* II, the ordinal number which opens the title-page strikes a note which is echoed elsewhere in the collection. For its expression, which mostly takes the form of pairs of opposites, we need look no further than the description of the contents:

bestehend in

einem Concerto nach Italienischen Gusto

und

einer Ouvertüre nach Französsischer Art

The antithesis encompasses forms (concerto and suite), styles (Italian and French), and, in the music itself, opposed tonalities (F major and B minor). This immediately raises the question as to why ordinal numbers are absent from the title-pages of the other sets. The absence of 'Erster Theil' from the tile-page of the Partitas (though 'Opus 1' does appear further down the page) can be explained simply on the hypothesis that Bach was not planning a sequel when he issued it, but the non-appearance of 'Vierter Theil' for the Goldberg Variations, reflected by the lack of any special emphasis on the number 4 in the music, is deliberate. We shall develop this theme further.

After the description of the contents (note the cryptic 'andere Gesaenge') comes the designation, which contains a second, more important clue to Bach's intentions. Again, the wording of the four title-pages is compared:

I   Denen Liebhabern
      zur Gemüths Ergoetzung verfertiget

II   Denen Liebhabern
      zur Gemüths Ergötzung verfertiget

III Denen Liebhabern,
      und besonders denen Kennern von dergleichen Arbeit
      zur Gemüths Ergezung verfertiget

IV Denen Liebhabern
      zur Gemüths Ergetzung verfertiget

The designation 'for connoisseurs and amateurs' was such a common feature of eighteenth-century title-pages that the additional phrase in the *Clavierübung* III title must have misled contemporary purchasers (particularly those who did not buy all four sets) just as it has misled scholars since. It is deliberately ambiguous; read as 'and especially for connoisseurs of such productions' it is no more than a well-tried formula familiar from dozens of other printed collections, but as 'and especially for those acquainted with such labour' it has a very different meaning. The 'labour' with which the discriminating reader is expected to be acquainted is, of course, the unravelling of the esoteric structure. This in turn points to the main motive which prompted Bach to this grandiose tour-de-force, which sheds new light on Bach's involvement in the musical polemics of the Leipzig of his day.

The only known printed review of *Clavierübung* III to date from Bach's lifetime is a brief notice which appeared in Lorenz Mizler's *Musikalische Bibliothek* early in 1740.[54] As an unsigned editorial it is presumably by Mizler, whose later transactions with Bach have already been mentioned in connection with the Bach gematria. After briefly reporting the publication, Mizler adds:

79

> The author has here given new proof that in this field of composition he is more practised and more fortunate than many others. No one will surpass him in it and few will be able to imitate him. The work is a powerful refutation of those who have made bold to criticise the composition of the Honourable Court Composer. [55]

This has been generally accepted as a reference to Bach's celebrated controversy with Johann Adolph Scheibe (1708 – 76) stemming from an article published in Scheibe's *Critischer Musikus* on 14 May 1737. [56] It is likely that Mizler's very choice of the word *critisiren* is an oblique taunt playing on the title of Scheibe's periodical. The illumination of the esoteric structure disposes of any idea that Mizler was referring to the set in a general sense as a demonstration of Bach's skill; on the contrary, it should be seen as a perfectly specific reply to Scheibe's criticisms. It is, indeed, Bach's single, decisive pronouncement on the censure Scheibe had levelled at him.

Here it is not necessary to tread the well-worn paths of the whole controversy aroused by Scheibe's original article, which was, it will be remembered, one of a series of ten critical sketches of prominent figures on the contemporary musical scene with the names of the subjects left blank as a puzzle for the reader. Instead we shall confine our attention to the various ways in which the *Clavierübung* bears on the controversy. There would appear to be three of them.

First, throughout the course of the dispute, which created a vigorous fluttering in the dovecots of Leipzig musical circles, more heat than light was generated by Scheibe's designation of Bach by the word *Musikant*, rather than by the more respectful *Musikus*. As Buelow has suggested, [57] this may in fact have been nothing more than a manifestation of the contemporary literary movement dedicated to the purification of the German language from foreign words, but it nevertheless gave great offence to Bach. His spokesman in the controversy, the Leipzig University rhetoric teacher Johann Abraham Birnbaum, expressed forcefully in his first pamphlet what must almost certainly have been Bach's own reaction to it:

> The term *Musikanten* is generally used for those whose principal achievement is a form of mere musical practice. They are employed for the purpose (indeed, they often devote themselves voluntarily to it) of bringing pieces written by others into sound by means of musical instruments. As a matter of fact, not even all the men of this sort, but only the humblest and meanest of them usually bear this name, so that there is hardly any difference between *Musikanten* and beer-fiddlers. [58]

For Bach, the choice of this term was not merely bad manners; in the intellectual and cultural system he represented, it was a violation of degree and thus an implicit perversion of the natural order.

This semantic point was one of the main threads running through the entire course of the debate. The use of the word *Musikant* was defended by Scheibe in his first counterblast to Birnbaum, attacked again by both Mizler and Birnbaum and mockingly persisted in by Scheibe throughout a venomous satire on Bach and his party which appeared in the *Critischer Musikus* on 2 April 1739. [59] Its refutation must undoubtedly have been one of Bach's aims in the esoteric structure of *Clavierübung* III. Moreover, the fact that the structure could be divined only by the suitably equipped reader was here the strongest card in his hand. It was clearly out of the question for him to publish written defences of his own music, but by presenting his reply in esoteric form he was able to give an ample demonstration of the breadth of his learning without exposing himself to the charge of vulgar self-advertisement. With the secret structure, Bach advances his claim to be, not a *Musikant*, not even merely a Cantor (his professional title) but a *Musicus*.

Secondly we have to consider the main burden of Scheibe's criticism, which was essentially the familiar charge that Bach's music was turgid (*schwülstig*), and old-fashioned, taxing the performer unnecessarily with its perverse difficulty and confusing the listener with its complex polyphonic textures:

> [Bach] would be the admiration of whole nations if he were more agreeable, if he did not take away the natural elements in his pieces by giving them a turgid and confused style, and if he did not darken their beauty by an excess of art. [60]

Scheibe adds a comparison with the poet Daniel Caspar von Lohenstein (1635 – 83) whose style was regarded in the intellectual circles of early eighteenth-century Leipzig as the epitome of bombastic, outmoded rhetoric. In an incidental reference published early in 1738[61] Scheibe repeats this criticism in a more specific form, maintaining that 'Bach's church compositions are always more artificial and laborious, but by no means of such effect, conviction, and reasonable reflection as the works of Telemann and Graun'.

Naturally, Scheibe was taken to task for this by Bach's supporters. In a brief editorial in the *Musikalische Bibliothek*, Mizler gives Scheibe the lie in a manner that, once again, probably gives a good idea of Bach's own reaction:

> Mr. Telemann and Mr. Graun are excellent composers, and Mr. Bach has written works of just the same quality, but if Mr. Bach at times writes the inner parts more fully than other composers, he has taken as his model the music of twenty or thirty years ago. He can write otherwise, however, when he wishes to. Anyone who heard the music that was performed by the students at the Easter Fair in Leipzig last year, in the Most High Presence of his Royal Majesty in Poland, which was composed by Kapellmeister Bach, must admit that it was written entirely in accordance with the latest taste, and was approved by everyone.[62]

Bach's own refutation, incorporated in the music of the *Clavierübung*, can be seen as a counterpart to Mizler's. The chorale preludes, as representative examples of Bach's mature manner, could indeed be said to recall 'the music of twenty or thirty years ago'. However, Bach proves the truth of Mizler's assertion that 'he can ... write otherwise when he wishes to' by including a single piece (the prelude) in the latest galant manner, and by pointedly placing it first in the collection.

Finally, Scheibe's whole attitude to Bach's music must be considered in the light of the intellectual climate of Bach's Leipzig, which was the scene of a vigorous clash between two opposed intellectual and cultural systems. One was enshrined in a staunchly conservative educational curriculum, solidly rooted in the doctrines of the Lutheran Church and the ideals of Renaissance humanism and represented by a faction among the university academics. They included the rhetorician Birnbaum, as well as the former St. Thomas's rector Johann Matthias Gesneir, whose edition of Quintilian's *Ars oratoria* Bach used as the basis for the Musical Offering in 1747. The other, to which Scheibe adhered, was the aesthetic outlook of the Enlightenment, of which Leipzig was one of the most important centres in Europe. The periodicals produced by Scheibe and Mizler were two among literally hundreds which sprung up in North German centres in the 1730s in emulation of their admired English models, the *Tatler* and the *Spectator*. Scheibe himself was a pupil of the Leipzig poetry professor Johann Christoph Gottsched, whose best-known work, *Versuch einer critischen Dichtkunst für die Deutschen* (1730), was then at the height of its influence. Gottsched himself was a populariser of the philosophy of Christian Wolff, the rationalist thinker whose systematically ordered series of treatises with titles beginning *Vernünftige Gedanken* . . . had won his ideas an enormous prestige in Leipzig university circles. The rigid form of naturalism prescribed for literature and theatre by Gottsched was eagerly extended to the musical field by Scheibe, whose view of the music of his day was governed by the ideals of Reason, Beauty and the imitation of Nature. All his criticisms of Bach reflect these habits of thought, which he applied to Bach's complex polyphony, fondness for contrapuntal artifice and awkward vocal writing. Any attentive reader of the original article will recognise the Enlightenment catchprases: 'if he did not take away the natural elements in his pieces' . . . 'if he did not darken their beauty by an excess of art' . . . 'turgidity has led them both [Bach and Lohenstein] from the natural to the artificial' . . . 'vainly employed, since they conflict with Reason'. Scheibe's censure of Bach's music in the Mattheson pamphlet for a lack of 'reasonable reflection' *(vernünftiges Nachdenken)* introduces another rationalist commonplace.

George Buelow has appealed persuasively for a reassessment of Scheibe as a major figure in eighteenth-century German musical thought,[63] and for a due recognition of his perceptiveness in realising that poetry, direct communication and human experience were to be the ideals of the music of the future. In the course of his observations, which are not, of course, directly concerned with *Clavierübung* III, Buelow puts his finger on the principal motive behind Bach's tour-de-force (see p. 79):

> Scheibe's forthright animosity towards anyone still believing that music was based on the mathematically orientated system of the liberal arts was the main reason for a number of critical attacks from a vocal group of enemies from his home town of Leipzig. It was above all Lorenz Mizler who led these attacks. When Scheibe wrote that no geometric, arithmetic, logarithmic or acoustic rules could contribute in the slightest to beauty in music, he was certainly thinking of Mizler. [64]

The classical system of the quadrivium is exactly what the esoteric structure of the *Clavierübung* is designed to uphold. It is a brilliant manifesto defending the classical view of music as a liberal art, grounded in the eternal verities of mathematics and the noble art of rhetoric, against the assults of those of the persuasion of Scheibe, who sought to relate it to poetry alone. As such it was close to the heart of Scheibe's arch-enemy Mizler, who produced a rival music periodical (the *Musikalische Bibliothek*) and whose *Societät der musikalischen Wissenschaften* had been formed in 1738, the year before the appearance of *Clavierübung* III.

Mizler, who lived from 1711 to 1778, was a man whose prodigiously wide interests included mathematics, philosophy, medicine and law as well as music. With his wide-ranging activities as lecturer, physician, librarian, mathematician and music journalist, he was almost the model of the humanist 'whole man'. Moreover the subject of his master's thesis, *Quod musica sit pars eruditionis philosophicae*, submitted to Leipzig University before his graduation on 4 March 1734, exactly reflects the ideals expressed by his formation of the society in 1738. Mizler had been a friend of Bach since his student days in the early 1730s. Bach's own membership of Mizler's society lasted from 4 June 1747 to his death, after which (in 1754) Mizler published in the final number of the Bibliothek the famous and informative *Nekrologie* (mostly by C.P.E. Bach and J.F. Agricola) which still serves as a valuable source of information about Bach's biography.

Mizler played a central organising role in Bach's campaign against Scheibe. As well as writing the two brief notices already quoted, he reprinted Birnbaum's first pamphlet *in toto* in the *Bibliothek*, and later published a brief summary of the whole controversy from a point of view favourable to Bach by Christoph Gottlieb Schröter.[66] In a sense, the broader aspects of the controversy served Mizler's ends more than Bach's. He almost certainly saw it as a pretext for one more of the series of attacks on Scheibe's aesthetic stance mounted by him in the *Bibliothek*. The personality and outlook of Lorenz Mizler is indeed so much a part of the history of Bach's *Clavierübung* III that another question is inevitably raised; did Mizler help Bach to plan the esoteric structure? After all, in the review quoted above he shows a general awareness of the aims of the collection, which in structure and scope could not be a more faithful reflection of his own wide learning, conservative philosophical position and dislike of Scheibe. Mizler's involvement would also help to explain what might otherwise seem a disproportionately crushing response on Bach's part to a meagre two paragraphs from Scheibe. When Mattheson attacked Bach in print for faulty text-declamation he seems to have taken no notice. It would be rash (indeed, probably wrong) to assume that Bach, a well-educated man and an excellent Latinist, could not have executed the design unaided, but it accords with Mizler's interests so exactly that we cannot ignore the small signs that he was privy to Bach's intentions. Mizler's profound influence on the small corpus of works produced by Bach in the late 1730's and 1740's seems to be emerging more and more clearly in the light of recent discoveries. Most of the works in which numerology and esoterics play a central role are connected in some way with the Mizler Society and the eager research into the music theory and philosophy of the ancients which dominates the pages of the *Musikalische Bibliothek*.

It is natural to ask whether Scheibe understood the esoteric structure, and here a survey of the (admittedly scanty) evidence suggests that he did not. His failure to mount any challenge to the blow aimed at him by Bach must itself be seen as negative evidence that he remained in ignorance of its meaning, at least within the immediate duration of the controversy. On 5 January 1740 he published, in an article not directedly concerned with the debate, the following remarks which should remind us that Scheibe retained his deep respect for Bach throughout the affair:

> Indeed, ask the great Bach, who has all musical artifices completely at his command, and whose admirable works one cannot see and hear without astonishment, if in the attainment of this great experience and skill he once thought of the mathematical relationship between the notes, and if in composing so many pieces he once took counsel from mathematics. [67]

These are hardly the words of a man who had grasped the intricacies of the *Clavierübung*. And in May 1740, when the collection had been in print for seven months, we find him vainly repeating his old accusation that Bach, unable to defend himself, was hiding behind his university friends. [68] Examples of this kind show the deadliness of the esoteric structure as a weapon against Scheibe; uncomprehending, and implicitly excluded from the ranks of 'Kenner von dergleichen Arbeit', he had been defeated without even realising it. It is not stretching imagination very far to suggest that he may have been the subject of a good deal of ridicule in the Bach circle. His original criticism of Bach had made no mention of mathematical devices, and this attack on Scheibe's reputation, going far beyond the immediate task of replying to his article, cannot but seem gratuitous.

We turn next to the secondary aim governing the organisation of the set, namely the provision of music for a complete Lutheran Sunday. The scheme is of course a figurative rather than a functionally liturgical one, though the set could be (and no doubt was) used as a store of suitable material by church organists in search of music for the Lutheran Mass and Vesper services. The question as to what prompted it is linked to the chronology of the set, and to its place in the whole series of *Clavierübung* volumes issued by Bach between 1731 and 1742. The year 1739 marked three Lutheran anniversaries. One of these, the Reformationsfest on 31 October, should surely be discounted as an annual event, but there remain the bicentenaries of Luther's sermon at St Thomas's on 25 May and the acceptance of the Augsburg Confessions by the Leipzig civic authority (not of the Augsburg Confessions themselves as Williams states) on 12 August. It is possible to maintain on present evidence that Bach, noticing the anniversaries, may have timed the public issue to coincide with either or both of them; indeed, the idea might derive support from the discovery by G.C. Butler[69] that Bach transferred the engraving from the Krügner factory in Leipzig to the more specialised control of Balthasar Schmid of Nuremberg. But it is harder to accept the theory (advanced by Leaver and supported by Williams) that Bach planned the liturgical aspects of the set with the religious anniversaries in mind. The overall planning exhibited by the three sets, and the existence of at least one famous precedent, seem to me to argue for the conclusion that the religious motive for *Clavierübung* III was inherent in the design of the whole series and was in Bach's mind from the early 1730s.

As already mentioned, the number of movements in each of the three sets (41, 14, 27) form Bach's mystic equation, in which the number 27, with its special position in Platonic and Jewish thought, coincides neatly with the *third* set. Another instance of overall planning is the progressive increase in the number of keyboard departments required; one for the first set, two for the second and three (two manuals and pedal) for the third. This strong hint that *Clavierübung* III was planned in advance as organ music is supported by an examination of likely models for the series. Bach scholars have, naturally enough, devoted much attention to this subject, and many have pointed to Bach's ownership of copies of Frescobaldi's *Fiori musicali* (1635) and de Grigny's *Premier livre d'orgue* (1699). Both of these have elements in common with Bach's scheme; Frescobaldi's collection comprises three organ masses and de Grigny's a single organ mass followed by versets for five office hymns. Further examples of the 'liturgical day' model come from other French organists (for example Le Bègue) and from the repertoire of Venetian and Bolognese collections of the *Messa e salmi* type (by Monteverdi, Grandi, Cazzati, Perti and others) of which Bach, as an enthusiastic admirer of the Italian *stile antico*, probably had some knowledge. From some of these Italian sets, also, Bach could have derived the stylistic antithesis between *stile antico* Mass and *stile nuovo* Vespers. But our clarification of Bach's liturgical aims focuses attention on a more direct model from the Protestant world. In another Part III – that of Scheidt's *Tabulatura nova* (1624) we find a precedent for several aspects of Bach's scheme. Scheidt's *Modus ludendi pleno organo pedaliter* and the following *Benedicamus Domino* from *Tabulatura nova* III are often cited as possible models for the six-part double pedal layout of Bach's *pedaliter* prelude on *Aus tiefer Not* (19) and the liturgical correspondences therefore come as no surprise.

Scheidt's *Tabulatura Nova* III is in principle a Protestant 'liturgical day' collection. It begins with Kyrie Dominicale and Gloria (the melodies differ from Bach's). Then it proceeds to nine Magnificat sets (the eight regular tones and the *tonus peregrinus*) and versets for six seasonal plainchant hymns. Next, the Vesper music completed, Scheidt returns to the Mass, supplying the Credo (*Wir glauben all'*) and, most interesting of all in the present connection, a six-verse setting of *Jesus Christus unser Heiland* actually labelled *Psalmus sub communione*. Scheidt's first verse, a rather pedestrian piece in a motet-like fugal texture, is quoted in Ex. 39; it is instructive to compare it with Bach's manualiter setting (22) whose liturgical implications it shares.

Scheidt's collection closes with the two double-pedal pieces mentioned above. The assumption that Bach knew Scheidt's work creates no problems. Walther's article on Scheidt, the length of which is a sure sign that he was still venerated in the North Germany of Bach's day, includes a contents list of all three parts which could only have been derived from first-hand knowledge.

All these factors suggest that the religious, if not the esoteric element in *Clavierübung* III was in Bach's mind from an early stage, most likely contemporary with the composition of *Clavier-*

Ex. 39. Scheidt, *Jesus Christus unser Heiland* (1624), bars 1 – 9

übung II (published 1735). The actual date of composition is
another matter. Here the first major limiting factor is the
surviving draft of a letter from Bach's cousin and secretary
Johann Elias Bach to Cantor Johann Wilhelm Koch in Bonne-
berg, soliciting subscriptions and predicting publication (over-
optimistically) in time for the forthcoming Easter Fair.[70] This
can only mean that by the date of the letter (10 January 1739) the
music was complete and the engraving far advanced. In the
above-mentioned bibliographic study, Butler stresses the need to
allow sufficient time for the laborious task of engraving in
estimating a composition date, and he himself favours '1737 or
even earlier'. In view of the connection with the Scheibe controversy, which the deliberate character and placing of the prelude
(if nothing else) seems to place beyond coincidence, I prefer a
dating in the second half of 1737, which would allow more than a
year for the engraving of the 45 plates produced in Leipzig before
the transfer to Schmid of Nuremberg. With its exceptional
length, and the intricacy of the underlying design, the collection
must have been the fruit of months of work even for a composer
of Bach's facility.

The overall organisation of the first three *Clavierübung* sets closes them off from the Goldberg Variations, a fact which, as we have seen, Bach signals by leaving the latter without a number, by making no use of the figure 4 in their internal planning, and perhaps by the handsome border design on the title page. The almost inevitable conclusion from this and the other factors mentioned above is that Bach conceived the variations as an afterthought to the series.

Yet the parallel title page, forming the clearest possible indication that Bach intended them to be seen in relation to the first three sets, invites the reader to look for an inner meaning there also. They certainly contain none of the esoteric fireworks of *Clavierübung* III, but in their design Bach contrived to add one simple, yet elegant, final twist to his formidable demonstration. In the nine ascending canons, each arrived at by a count of three variations, Bach presents an allegory on the music of the spheres, adding the last element of the quadrivium (astronomy) to the three shown in *Clavierübung* III.

Support for this interpretation, which should surprise nobody acquainted with the rich classical symbolism of much baroque art, comes from various quarters. No musical form was more steeped in this symbolism than the canon, and Bach himself made repeated use of it in the Musical Offering, in the miscellaneous dedication canons, and in the fourteen canons with which he 'signed' his personal copy of the Goldberg Variations themselves. There is no need to multiply universally familiar examples, but the fact that Bach could praise Frederick the Great with a spiral canon rising through the six whole-tones of the octave and inscribed *Ascendenteque Modulatione ascendat Gloria Regis* should in itself prove that such things were part of Bach's habits of thought.

Secondly, the cosmological interpretation fits the Goldberg Variations neatly into the overall design of the four sets. In the first three sets Bach gives a demonstration of the age-old lesson of the magic 'count of three' by following two sets of purely artistic content with a creative 'explosion' of esoteric symbolism in the third. In the Goldberg Variations he shows the application of this. Every time the number three is counted out in variations the reader finds a canon which marks a rung on the planetary ladder, the interval of the canon widening by degrees from the unison (Earth) to the ninth (fixed stars). A tenth count reveals the quod-libet, a perfect expression of convivial mirth and, in the present context, an illustration of the harmonising and cheering effect of music. It may be added that the cosmological scheme has the merit of making equally good sense inside or outside the context of the whole series.

Bach's choice of variation form is probably explained by Pythagorean – Platonic cosmology and philosophy. The theme could conveniently be seen as the Platonic Idea, first heard in its pristine form, then obscured by the 'muddy vesture of decay' (the variations) and finally, following the soul's ascent to nine successive degrees of perfection, re-established as before, by the *da capo* of the Aria at the end.

Even the key of the Goldberg Variations may be connected with the cosmological allegory. The famous source passage in the tenth book of Plato's *Republic* does not name the notes sung by the sirens of the eight celestial spheres, specifying only that they all belonged to one mode, but later Neoplatonist writers were not slow to add their own speculations. In *De institutione musica* I 27 Boethius quotes Cicero's opinion that the outer spheres, because of their faster revolution, produce the highest notes. He then suggests that the notes from *proslambanomenos* [A] to *mese* [a] in the diatonic genus could be assigned to the eight celestial spheres to produce the supernal diapason. In present-day notation, this produces the following equivalents:

Moon	A
Mercury	B
Venus	c
Sun	d
Mars	e
Jupiter	f
Saturn	g
Fixed stars	a

This scheme, which adopts the by then traditional ordering whereby the sun was placed in the middle for astrological reasons, was adopted by Gafurius (1496) for his famous serpent diagram and quoted by Morley (1597). If the interval of each of Bach's nine canons is taken in relation to the keynote G, the result is an excellent correspondence with Boethius's order. In Ex. 40 F♮ is taken for Variation 21, which is in the minor:

Ex. 40.

When Bach searched through the 1725 Anna Magdalena Notebook he may have had a specific reason for wanting a piece in G major, the only key suitable as a basis for his cosmological scheme.

Reverting finally to *Clavierübung* III, all that remains is to give some brief indications of its relationship to its cultural background. It is hardly necessary to state that the concept of the esoteric work of art with a clearly defined outer face for the many (*Liebhaber*) and an inner face for the initiate few (*Kenner von dergleichen Arbeit*) was enshrined in a long-standing tradition to which Bach's design formed a conscious tribute. It was associated especially with the Renaissance humanist thought of which the educational system of Bach's Germany was an artificially late survival. The concept of the world's 'Janus face' with one aspect appearing to the common man and a second accessible only to those with special wisdom or learning held a peculiar fascination for the Renaissance mind. It was applied to fields as diverse as philosophy, biblical exegesis, alchemy, painting, poetry and magic. Its purposes could include self-preservation for those harbouring heterodox views on religion, politics or astronomy, or praise (imputing special understanding or wisdom to the person praised). The latter purpose, as we now know, was followed by Bach in composing the Musical Offering. However, its original object, for which its practitioners drew support from classical antiquity, early Neoplatonic philosophy and certain passages in the Bible,[71] was to propagate sacrosanct ideas while at the same time concealing them from the profane eye. Pico della Mirandola, one of the major figures among the fifteenth-century Florentine Neoplatonists and a key figure in the development of Renaissance humanist thought, observed that mysteries should be spoken of in words that are 'published and not published' (*editos esse et non editos*).[72]

Anything approaching an adequate summary of the tradition of humanist artifice to which Bach's *Clavierübung* III belongs is beyond the scope of the present study. The reader may be safely referred to an excellent account by Edward Lowinsky[73] embracing many fields of artistic and intellectual achievement and encompassing Pico, Erasmus, Pomponazzi, Rabelais, Brueghel, Marot and even Shakespeare. One example cited by Lowinsky is worth mentioning here as a striking instance of the continuity of the tradition. A surviving Latin poem by Joannes Bockenrodt in praise of the Emporor Ferdinand I

> reveals its peculiar structure by rows of conspicuous capital letters wandering through the different lines in geometrical patterns. If one reads the letters arranged along these patterns, one arrives at another, the 'inner' poem, drawing out the patterns, one comes to the innermost sanctum and finds four hexagons in the form of a cross, eight equilateral quadrangles, and one square, each of which has a symbolic meaning: the four hexagons in the form of a cross signify the four Gospels and the four kingdoms over which Ferdinand reigned and in which he was to defend the Gospel; the eight equilateral quadrangles represent the eight grades of the beatitude through which he was to come to the Kingdom of God, and the square is a symbol of his strong, solid, and constant personality.[74]

One spectacular discovery in the field of Renaissance allegory and double meaning made since these words were written is the fantastically complex cosmological allegory behind the surface of Spenser's *The Faerie Queene*.[75]

The survival of these highly conservative modes of thought in the Leipzig of the 1730s is, as already stated, a measure of the resilience of a traditional educational system and throws the issues surrounding the cultural warfare waged by Scheibe and his party against elements in the academic establishment into still sharper relief. As we know, Scheibe's party gradually won their victory in the artistic sphere, and Bach's *Clavierübung* stands as one of the last moments to a system of cultural values that had almost had its day. However, this in itself does nothing to devalue Bach's achievement, which was to enrich posterity with a unique and brilliantly conceived work of esoteric art.

Notes

1. J.P. Kirnberger, *Die Kunst des reinen Satzes* ... Vol. II (Berlin and Konigsberg, 1776 – 9), extracts in *Bach-Dokumente* Vol. III p. 221: P. Williams, *The Organ Works of J.S. Bach* (vols 1 – 2, Cambridge, 1980). The relevant sections of Williams are Vol. I pp. 184 – 91 (prelude and fugue), *ibid.* pp. 321 – 27 (Duetti) and Vol. II pp. 175 – 225 (chorale preludes).

2. The earliest of the Catechism chorales appeared in the *Enchiridion* (Erfurt, 1524) and the so-called *Wittenberg Gesangbuch* (Wittenberg, 1524). They were progressively added to in later collections.

3. Prescribed for liturgical use in *Leipziger Kirchen-Andachten* (Leipzig, 1694) p. 11 and printed monophonically in the *Neu Leipziger Gesangbuch* (1682) pp. 423ff. (see modern edn. in NBA Serie IV Band 4, preface). In Bach's Leipzig the Latin and German Kyrie were sung on alternate Sundays.

4. First prescribed for liturgical use in the *Neu Leipziger Gesangbuch*, *ibid*.

5. The text employed for the present article is that given in H.H. Borcherdt and G. Merz (ed.) *Martin Luther Ausgewählte Werke,* (1948 –) Vol. III, pp. 167 – 185. Like Bach's esoteric structure, it is based on the enlarged version first arrived at in the edition of 1531.

6. G. Rhau (pub.) *Bicinia gallica, latina, germanica* (2 sets, Wittenberg, 1545), C. Othmayr, *Bicinia sacra* (Nuremberg, 1547), M. Praetorius, *bicinia* based on chorale melodies from several of his published collections (see article on Praetorius in *The New Grove*).

7. Plato (ed. and tr. P. Shorey), *Republic* (*The Loeb Classical Library*, Cambridge, Mass., 1930), Vol. I pp. 247 – 49.

8. Other writers who confirm this conventional interpretation include Ornithoparcus (*Micrologus*, 1517) who cites Cassiodorus and Caelius for the view that 'the Dorian Mood is the bestower of wisdom and causer of chastity' and 'the Phrygian causeth wars and enflameth fury' (Dowland's translations). See also the passage from Aristotle's *Politics* reproduced in O. Strunk, *Source Readings in Music History* (New York, 1950) pp. 13 – 24.

9. e.g. J.G. Walther, *Praecepta der musicalischen Composition* (MS, 1708) and J. Mattheson, *Der vollkommene Capellmeister* (Hamburg, 1739).

10. U. Kirkendale, 'The Source for Bach's Musical Offering', *Journal of the American Musicological Society* XXXIII (1980) pp. 88 – 141.

11. Author's translations throughout.

12. The edition consulted for this study is that of the *Neue Bach Ausgabe* Serie IV Band 4, though not every detail of the layout in the music examples corresponds with that edition. I have also consulted a copy of the original engraving preserved in the British Library (shelf-mark K 10 a 2).

13. Two examples are the *Sinfonia* and closing chorale of the Christmas Oratorio Cantata II, and the opening aria of Cantata 151 (*Süsser Trost, mein Jesus kommt*).

14. W. Emery (ed.), *J.S. Bach, Organ Works*, Vol. VI (Novello), preface.

15. J. Chailley, *Les chorals pour orgue de J.S. Bach* (Paris, 1974) p. 262.

16. Kirkendale, *op. cit.*, p. 107.

17. *ibid.*, p. 98.

18. The passage is worth comparing with Var. 25 of the Goldberg Variations, an unmistakable example of Bach's instrumental aria style.

19. Matthew 3, 16 – 17, Mark 1, 10 – 11, Luke 3, 22, John 1, 32.

20. Boethius, *De musica* I, 2 (see Strunk, *op. cit.*, pp. 84 – 85).

21. For a discussion of the *stile antico* in Bach's *Clavierübung* III see C. Wolff, *Das stile antico in der Musik Johann Sebastian Bachs* (Wiesbaden, 1968). The *stile antico* music in the Mass preludes is usually related to Bach's ownership of a copy of Frescobaldi's *Fiori musicali*, though to the present writer the resemblance seems general rather than specific.

22. S.K. Heiniger Jr., *Touches of Sweet Harmony* (San Marino, 1974), pp. 71 – 145.

23. F.M. Cornford, *Plato's Cosmology* (London, 1937).

24. J.H. Waszink (ed.), *Timaeus a Calcidio translatus commentarioque instructus* (London and Leyden, 1962).

25. See Macrobius (tr. and ed. W.H. Stahl), *Commentary on the Dream of Scipio* (New York, 1952), p. 108.

26. The schematic arrangement of time signatures has been noticed, but to brush it aside as 'progressive triple time' (Williams, *op. cit.*, Vol. I, p. 180) is to miss the point.

27. See E. Werner, 'The Mathematical Foundation of Philippe de Vitry's Ars Nova', *Journal of the American Musicological Society* IX (1956), pp. 128 – 32.

28. See R. Bragard (ed.), *Jacobi Leodensis Speculum Musicae,* (American Institute of Musicology, 1955 –), Vol. I, p. 223 and Vol. III, p. 100.

29. N. Oresme (tr. and ed. E. Grant), *De proportionibus de proportionum* (Madison etc., 1966), p. 234.

30. See Mattheson, *op. cit.*, p. 187 and Bach's own canon *Trias Harmonica* (BWV 1072). The major triad was regarded with veneration by theorists; Christopher Simpson (*The Division Violist*, 1659) was not alone in comparing the three notes to the three Persons of the Trinity.

31. The sanction for alternating the Latin Kyrie with the German trope *Kyrie Gott Vater in Ewigkeit* is given in the *Leipziger Kirchen-Staat* (Leipzig, 1710) p. 5.

32. See C. S. Terry, *J. S. Bach Cantata Texts* (London, 1926) p. 33 and G. Stiller, *Johann Sebastian Bach und das Leipziger gottesdienstliche Leben seiner Zeit* (Kassel, 1970) pp. 103 – 4. The principal choir, which sang in St Thomas's and St Nicholas's on alternate Sundays, sang a figured setting in Latin.

33. The fact that, from this viewpoint, Bach's esoteric structure indicates two alternative Kyrie-Gloria pairs could be seen as support for the view that Bach intended the greater and lesser Kyrie cycles at least to represent Luther's two alternative forms of German Mass.

34. Augustine (tr. and ed. D. S. Wiesen), *The City of God Against the Pagans* (*Loeb Classical Library*, 6 vols, London etc., 1957 –), Vol. III, pp. 552 – 7.

35. Stahl, *op. cit.* See also V. Hopper, *Mediaeval Number Symbolism* (New York, 1938) pp. 52 – 3.

36. *ibid.*, pp. 34 – 5.

37. *ibid.*, pp. 104 – 5.

38. Cornford, *op. cit.*, p. 99.

39. *An Apology for Poetry*, quoted in M.H. Abrams, *The Mirror and the Lamp* (Oxford, 1955), p. 14.

40. F. Dietrich, 'J.S. Bachs Orgelchoral und seine geschichtlichen Würzeln', *Bach-Jahrbuch*, XXVI (1929), pp. 1 – 89.

41. R.A. Leaver, 'Bach's Clavierübung III: Some Historical and Theological Considerations', *Organ Yearbook*, VI (1975), pp. 17 – 32.

42. J. J. Quantz (tr. and ed. E.R. Reilly), *On Playing the Flute* (London, 1966), p. 103.

43. H. Keller, *Die Orgelwerke Bachs* (Leipzig, 1948), p. 207.

44. *Neue Deudsche Geistliche Gesaenge für die gemeinen Schulen* (Wittenberg, 1544); modern edition in *Denkmäler Deutscher Tonkunst* (Series I, Vol. 34, p. 106).

45. Another source of information on this point is the *Leipziger Kirchen-Staat* (see Terry, *op. cit.*, p. 48). Here *Jesus Christus unser Heiland* is the first of six chorales prescribed for singing *sub communione*.

46. In the *Leipziger Kirchen-Staat* the singing of a Latin motet is prescribed to precede the chorales if the number of communicants is large (see Stiller, *op. cit.*, p. 114). This could be conveniently identified with Bach's 'die Music'.

47. Luther, *Werke*, Vol. III, p. 177.

48. *ibid.*, p. 182.

49. A startlingly close parallel is the diagram of the ground-plan of Milan Cathedral published in an edition of Vitruvius' *Ten Books* in 1521 and shown in N. Pennick, *Sacred Geometry* (Wellingborough, 1980), p. 107. It

is based on six geometric figures; three concentric circles, square, cross and hexagon.

50. R. Headlam Wells, 'Number Symbolism in the Renaissance Lute Rose', *Early Music*, VIII (1980), pp. 32 – 42. See Heiniger *op. cit.*, p. 178 for similar manifestations in the Renaissance 'dancing maze'.

51. P. Cowen, *Rose Windows* (London, 1979).

52. G. Butler, 'Ordering Problems in J.S. Bach's *Art of Fugue* Resolved', *The Musical Quarterly*, LXIX (1983), pp. 44 – 61.

53. F. Smend, 'Johann Sebastian Bach bei seinem Namen gerufen', *Bach-Studien*, ed. C. Wolff (Kassel, 1969).

54. Reproduced in *Bach-Dokumente*, Vol. II, pp. 386 – 87.

55. Translation from H.T. David and A. Mendel, *The Bach Reader* (rev. edn., New York, 1966), p. 235.

56. *Bach-Dokumente*, Vol. II, p. 286 – 88.

57. G. Buelow, 'In Defence of J.A. Scheibe against J.S. Bach', *Proceedings of the Royal Musical Association*, CI (1974 – 5), pp. 85 – 100.

58. J.A. Birnbaum, *Unpartheyische Anmerkungen über eine bedenckliche Stelle in dem sechsten Stück des Critischen Musicus* (Leipzig, 1738) reproduced in *Bach-Dokumente* Vol. II, pp. 296 – 396 (English translation in *The Bach Reader*, pp. 239 – 47).

59. Reproduced in *Bach-Dokumente*, Vol. II, pp. 360 – 63.

60. Translation from *The Bach Reader*, p. 238, slightly adapted following Buelow.

61. J.A. Scheibe, *Sendeschreiben an Sr. Hock-Edl. Herrn Capellmeister Mattheson* (Hamburg, 1738) reproduced in *Bach-Dokumente*, Vol. II, p. 307.

62. *Musikalische Bibliothek* (1738, Part VI) reproduced in *Bach-Dokumente*, Vol. II, p. 336.

63. Buelow, *op. cit.*

64. *ibid.*, p. 98.

65. Reproduced in *Bach-Dokumente*, Vol. III, pp. 80 – 93.

66. *Musikalische Bibliothek* (1746, Part II), reproduced in *Bach-Dokumente*, Vol. II, pp. 432 – 33.

67. Reproduced in *Bach-Dokumente*, Vol. II, p. 379 (author's translation).

68. See *Bach-Dokumente*, Vol. II, p. 383[n].

69. 'Leipziger Stecher in Bachs Originaldrucken', *Bach-Jahrbuch*, LXVI (1980), pp. 9 – 26.

70. *Bach-Dokumente*, Vol. II, p. 335.

71. e.g. Exodus 34, 33 – 5, Matthew 13, 10 – 13.

72. Quoted in E. Wind, *Pagan Mysteries in the Renaissance*, (rev. edn., Oxford, 1967), p. 11. The opening chapter of this book gives a brilliant account of the philosophical background to Renaissance esoterics.

73. E. Lowinsky, *Secret Chromatic Art in the Netherlands Motet* (New York, 1946) ch. 7.

74. *ibid.*, pp. 165 – 66.

75. The standard work on this subject is A. Fowler, *Spenser and the Numbers of Time* (London, 1964).